THE BASEBALL
HALL OF SHAME 3

Books by Bruce Nash and Allan Zullo

The Baseball Hall of Shame
The Baseball Hall of Shame 2
The Baseball Hall of Shame 3
The Football Hall of Shame

Published by POCKET BOOKS

THE BASEBALL HALL OF SHAME 3

Bruce Nash and Allan Zullo

Bernie Ward, Curator

PUBLISHED BY POCKET BOOKS NEW YORK

*This book is dedicated to baseball fans everywhere,
with hopes that your lives will always be filled
with more fame than shame.*

An *Original* publication of POCKET BOOKS

 POCKET BOOKS, a division of Simon & Schuster, Inc.,
1230 Avenue of the Americas, New York, N.Y. 10020

ISBN: 0-671-63386-4

First Pocket Books trade paperback printing March, 1987

10   9   8   7   6   5   4   3   2

Printed the the U.S.A.

ACKNOWLEDGMENTS

We wish to thank all the fans, players, coaches, and sportswriters who contributed nominations.

We are especially grateful to those players, past and present, who shared a few laughs with us as they recounted the inglorious moments that earned them a place in The Baseball Hall of SHAME.

This book couldn't have been completed without the outstanding research of Al Kermisch or the kindness of Dick Cohen, president of the Sports Bookshelf in Ridgefield, Connecticut, who allowed us access to his wonderful collection of baseball books.

We also appreciate the special efforts of Jackie Blum, Bill Borst, Bob Broeg, Bob Brown, Bill Carle, Phil Collier, Joe Gallagher, Paul Hagen, Bill Haig, Duffy Jennings, Lloyd Johnson, Charles Kagan, Clay Kemp, Ed Kranepool, Bud Lea, Phil Lowry, Bob McConnell, Tom Mee, Glenn Miller, Steve Nadel, Mike Ortman, Rick Plumlee, Danny Thompson, Bob Weiss, Toby Zwickel, and the Honorable Thomas Vezzetti, mayor of Hoboken, New Jersey.

Our lineup wouldn't be such a winner without our two greatest stars, Sophie Nash and Kathy Zullo.

CONTENTS

LEADING OFF

There was never any doubt that we would write a third volume of *The Baseball Hall of SHAME*. We couldn't possibly cram more than 100 years of baseball shame into only two volumes because America's national pastime provides us with a never-ending supply of wacky moments. From the 1986 season alone, we inducted more than a dozen new players whose rib-tickling boners earned them enshrinement in Blooperstown.

Our ongoing research has been complemented by the hundreds of nominations that we have received from readers—and by the overwhelming cooperation of players and team officials who have graciously assisted us. When our first book, *The Baseball Hall of SHAME*, was published in the spring of 1985, many members of the baseball establishment reacted with cool detachment—and in some cases, outright anger. But once they had a chance to read the book and enjoy the true, humorous stories about the game we all love, their attitude changed dramatically. All of the new induct-ees we spoke with laughed about their shameful moments of infamy. It didn't matter if they were big stars or not.

Before a spring training game in West Palm Beach, Florida, in 1986, Willie Stargell, a coach with the Atlanta Braves, spotted us on the field and demanded that we give him a copy of *The Baseball Hall of SHAME 2*—which we did—because he had made it into the book. (As you may recall, Stargell was inducted for trying to call time out after his slide on a rare attempted steal came up twenty feet short of the bag.) After reading about himself in the book, Willie hustled off to the clubhouse and proudly showed the other Braves his shameful incident in print.

At the New York Yankees' spring training clubhouse in Fort Lauderdale, infielder Dale Berra said he was "delighted" by his induction (for the time when he and teammate Bobby Meacham were thrown out at the plate on the same play). Don Mattingly, whose locker was next to Berra's, told us, "There's a lot more shame that I could tell you guys about." Although he didn't reveal any at the time, we found a good reason to induct him—along with Berra again—in this book.

Many former players who had long been forgotten were delighted to hear they had been selected for induction. At least, they figured, they would be remembered for something—even if it was an embarrassing but funny moment. Upon confirming his day of ignobility, former journeyman relief pitcher Will McEnaney said, "This is the first time I've made it into the Hall of Shame since the time I went out with an ugly girl."

Former New York Met Ron Swoboda—who once told reporters during his playing days, "Why am I wasting so much dedication on such a mediocre career?"—finally discovered the answer. When he learned he made it into *The Baseball Hall of SHAME 3*, Swoboda declared, "I earned it!"

One of the game's all-time flakes, John Lowenstein, who joins such other Hall of Shamers as Ping Bodie, Boots Poffenberger, and Buckshot Brown, told us, "It's an honor to be in there with so many great names. Just make sure you spell my name right."

To be truthful, not everyone in baseball was thrilled to have made the Hall of Shame. When we personally handed Baltimore Orioles manager Earl Weaver a copy of *The Baseball Hall of SHAME 2*, he smiled and thanked us. "By the way, Earl, you're in the book," we said. His smile turned to a scowl. "For what?" he asked. When he learned it was for being ejected from both ends of a doubleheader, he turned his back on us and stalked off. But he kept the book.

That's more than could be said for Yankees manager Lou Piniella. Before a spring training game in 1986, we handed him a copy of *The Baseball Hall of SHAME*. Piniella laughed as he scanned the pages, especially the chapter "Odious Owners," which included his boss, George Steinbrenner. But Piniella slammed the book shut and gave it back to us after our list of Yankee managers fired by Steinbrenner concluded with "to be continued."

Then there was the reaction of star catcher Ted Simmons, who was tracked down in a hotel room in San Francisco. We unintentionally woke him up to talk about one of his most embarrassing moments which is detailed in this book. Ted reluctantly confirmed the incident and then grumbled, "This is not my favorite way of starting off the day."

Many of today's biggest stars are dishonored in this book, including Rickey Henderson, Wade Boggs, Jim Rice, Steve Garvey, Pete Rose, Dave Righetti, Reggie Jackson, Goose Gossage, Dave Winfield, and Steve Sax, along with the stars of the recent past such as Willie Mays, Don Drysdale, Frank Robinson, Warren Spahn, Lou Brock, and Tim McCarver.

The grand old game will continue to produce hilarious happenings and ignoble incidents on and off the field. And we will be there to chronicle these embarrassing moments. We won't play favorites. We will dishonor both the superstars and the bozos. As our motto says: "Fame *and* shame are part of the game."

OPENING DAZE

As everyone knows, the most important day of the year is Opening Day. There is no surer sign of spring, no clearer harbinger of our recovery from cabin fever. Unfortunately, the season opener is also a red-letter day for those afflicted with a bizarre type of spring fever that has caused players, fans, and even presidents to make complete fools of themselves. For "The Most Embarrassing Moments on Opening Day," The Baseball Hall of SHAME inducts the following:

Frankie Zak

Shortstop • Pittsburgh, N.L. • April 17, 1945

No one wanted to be in Frankie Zak's shoes after his untied shoelace cost his team an Opening Day victory.

Playing against the Reds in Cincinnati, the Pittsburgh Pirates were leading 1–0 in the top of the fifth inning when Zak beat out a bunt, putting runners on first and second. Moments later, just as Reds pitcher Bucky Walters went into his stretch, Zak noticed that his shoe was untied and called time. First base umpire Ziggy Sears waved his arms in an attempt to halt play but his signal wasn't seen by Walters, plate umpire George Barr, or batter Jim Russell.

Walters threw the pitch and Russell clouted the ball into the right-field bleachers for what he thought was a three-run homer. "I was feeling pretty damn good about it," Russell recalled. "But when I got to first base, Ziggy was holding up his hands and shaking his head and telling me to go back to the plate. I said, 'What the hell is wrong?' And he said, 'I called time, Jim. The homer doesn't count.'

"I hollered and [Pirates manager] Frankie Frisch argued, but there was nothing we could do about it. Through it all, Zak just stood on first shaking his head in shame."

Once Zak had tied his shoe, Russell returned to the plate. But he couldn't duplicate his feat, although he did hit a single to drive in the Pirates' only run of the inning. That was little consolation for Pittsburgh. Scoring only one run instead of three—thanks to Zak's untied shoe—the Pirates went on to lose 7–6 in 11 innings.

"I'll always remember that we lost a game that we should have won on that homer," said Russell. "Zak kept apologizing but I couldn't get too mad at him." The same couldn't be said for their manager.

The next day in the Pittsburgh clubhouse, Frisch walked over to Zak's locker and handed him a package. "What's this?" asked the surprised shortstop.

"Buckle-up shoes," Frisch replied with a scowl. "I don't want to see you out there calling time to tie your damn shoes anymore!"

Rest Room Invaders

Busch Stadium • April 8, 1986

The 1986 season opener in St. Louis saw the most shameful example ever of relief bitching. Women fans were so fed up with the long lines in their rest rooms that they stormed a men's bathroom and commandeered the toilets.

The game at Busch Stadium between the Cardinals and the visiting Chicago Cubs drew a standing-room-only crowd—and so did the women's rest rooms. There simply weren't enough of them. Lines reached near-colossal proportions, blocking aisles, ramps, and walkways. Nearly 200 frustrated female spectators who were waiting outside one of the women's bathrooms during the fourth inning missed all the scoring by their hometown Cards, who defeated the Cubs 2–1.

Midway through the game, a group of impatient and uncomfortable distaff fans could no longer control themselves—or their bladders. They decided to take swift action. Since the men had something the women wanted—toilets— the female fans launched an invasion of a men's rest room. The women went to the door and announced to the men inside that they should leave so the female fans could use the stalls—temporarily, of course.

"We had to take over the men's room," said one woman. "Their lines were shorter and we just had to go."

Added another raider, "It was either go in the men's room or go in the line."

Some of the men couldn't believe their bathroom had been taken over by women. "Man, you're not safe anywhere anymore," complained one rousted male. "What's the world coming to?"

Said his disgruntled buddy, "I offered to share my urinal with one of the gals, but she told me to buzz off. I was just trying to be hospitable. After all, this was a *men's* john."

Jeffrey Wehling, a spokesman for the Civic Center Corp., which owns Busch Stadium, said more women's bathrooms were being built to alleviate the problem. He added that the Opening Day rest room siege was caused by a combination of a sellout crowd and the fact that "women take longer than men in the bathroom."

Ebbets Field Ceremonies

April 17, 1934

For decades, baseball clubs have staged innocuous Opening Day ceremonies without encountering any problems. The introduction of the players, the flag raising, and the tossing out of the first ball by a famous person are routine matters. Routine, that is, everywhere but in Ebbets Field, home of the Brooklyn Dodgers.

As the players from both teams were about to parade onto the field for the start of the 1934 season, a fan hurled a lengthy string of lighted firecrackers that sent the players scurrying. They finally regrouped and marched with some trepidation through the swirling clouds of smoke.

Suddenly, one of the flags festooning an upper box of the ball park caught on fire and dropped blazing into the grandstand below. Fortunately, the fans scattered and no harm was done except to the flag.

Through these unusual, nerve-racking events sat Borough President Raymond Ingersoll, who was on hand to throw out the first ball. But the umpires, club officials, and players forgot all about him. The umpire shouted, "Play ball!" So they did.

Dodgers pitcher Van Mungo fired a strike. The 1934 season was under way. Or was it? Someone finally remembered the borough president. So the pitch was discounted and Ingersoll was allowed to throw out the first ball, even though by this time it was really the second ball.

Once again the game was about to begin. But then another fan got into the act by hurling a huge ripe lemon onto the field—the best way to sum up the Opening Day ceremonies at Ebbets Field.

Chicago White Sox

April 10, 1979

The performance of the Chicago White Sox in their home opener was so atrocious that owner Bill Veeck offered every fan in the ball park free admission to the next game.

"Give us another chance, please," pleaded Veeck after 41,043 spectators suffered through 40-degree weather to watch the Sox get blown out 10–2 by the supposedly inept Toronto Blue Jays. Sox pitchers issued 12 walks while the defense failed to make the easy plays. A five-run Toronto ninth was triggered when second baseman Alan Bannister, a late-inning defensive replacement, muffed a simple grounder. Trying to explain away his miscue, · Bannister said, "My glove must have been frozen."

Following his team's ghastly Opening Day flop, an embarrassed Veeck confessed: "We stunk the joint out." Refusing to believe the Sox were as bad as they played, he announced, "Anybody who produces a raincheck, or a reasonable facsimile, is our guest tomorrow free of charge."

But the fans weren't dumb. They knew a lousy team when they saw one. Although Veeck tried to give away the next game at the gate, few Sox fans wanted it. Only 2,220 forgiving rooters took advantage of his offer, joining a meager 1,205 others who paid—and later wished they hadn't—to get in.

But if Veeck couldn't give the game away, the White Sox relief corps could. They failed to hold on to a 7–2 lead, giving up six runs in the eighth inning as Chicago lost for the second straight day, 9–7. The best things in life might be free—but not for the Sox that day at Comiskey Park.

Ronald Reagan

President • United States of America • April 7, 1986

President Reagan threw the wildest first ball in major league history.

To open the new season at Baltimore's Memorial Stadium, Reagan stepped onto the field to throw out the ceremonial first pitch. This seemed like a simple enough task. After all, during his acting days, Reagan portrayed Hall of Fame pitcher Grover Cleveland Alexander in the film *The Winning Team.*

But Reagan acted like a losing pitcher on Opening Day, 1986. With reporters, photographers, and dignitaries on the field watching him, the president peered at Baltimore Orioles catcher Rick Dempsey, wound up, and threw the ball—ten feet over Dempsey's head! Predictably, Reagan's pitch also sailed far to the right.

The crowd roared with laughter as the embarrassed leader of the greatest nation in the world asked for a second chance. He made the most of it by throwing a strike to Dempsey.

"On the first throw, the president said he was afraid he would hit one of the reporters," explained the catcher. "I said, 'Go ahead, that's no loss.' But he doesn't look at it that way. He needs all the votes he can get."

Don Drysdale

Pitcher • Los Angeles, N.L. • April 7, 1969

Several pitchers have the ignominious distinction of seeing their very first pitch on Opening Day whacked for a home run. But Don Drysdale one-upped them all.

In the curtain-raiser for the 1969 season in Cincinnati, the Los Angeles Dodgers tabbed Drysdale, their ace sidewinder, to take the mound against the Reds. The fourteen-year veteran had toed the rubber in many Opening Day games, but none started more ingloriously than this one.

Pete Rose was the very first batter to face Drysdale. The fastball hurler looked in at catcher Tom Haller for the sign. Then he wound up and fired his first pitch of the new season. The ball never reached Haller. Rose leaped on the pitch and drilled it over the left-field wall for a home run. Drysdale shook his head and mumbled something to himself about this being a hell of a way to start the year.

But the worst was yet to come as Bobby Tolan, the next batter, stepped up to the plate. Drysdale wound up and let fly a fastball. But it wasn't fast enough. Tolan belted the pitch into the right-field bleachers for another four-bagger. Incredibly, Drysdale's first two pitches of the new season turned out to be gopher balls. Even more grating, neither batter had hit a homer during all of spring training.

Overcoming a bad case of *déjà vu,* Drysdale settled down and didn't give up any more runs as the Dodgers won 3–2. Afterward, Drysdale was asked if the homers surprised him. "Let's just say they woke me up real quick," he said. "No one has ever started a season like that before."

Toronto Blue Jays Fans

April 14, 1986

The scene was set for the most perfect Opening Day in Toronto Blue Jay history—but some 2,000 unruly fans in the cheap seats did their best to spoil it.

Exhibition Stadium's name took on an ominous new meaning as it became the site of one of the sorriest exhibitions of rowdiness ever seen during a home opener.

The idiot fringe among the 43,587 spectators acted as if they were escapees from a mass breakout at the local asylum. Throughout the game between the Blue Jays and Baltimore Orioles, waves of crazies leaped from their bleacher seats behind the outfield fence. They darted across the field to the first-base stands as beleaguered security guards and groundskeepers chased them. The most important statistics were not runs and hits but arrests (35) and ejections (126).

Nothing seemed to faze the maddening crowd. The rabble-rousers were not deterred by either the security guards' hard tackling or the announcement over the public address system that the umpires were considering forfeiting the game to Baltimore. The mob continually interrupted a fine pitching duel between the Jays' Doyle Alexander and the O's Mike Boddicker. By the seventh inning, Baltimore manager Earl Weaver was so fed up that he played the game under formal protest.

Later, he stung the Blue Jay fans with the worst possible insult of all—he claimed they were more disorderly than those who inhabit the Bronx Zoo, otherwise known as Yankee Stadium. "I've never seen that many fans take to the field during a game," Weaver said. "Why they do it, I don't know. But to jump on the field, get tackled and whacked like some of them did, and then get hit for a $100 fine, it's crazy."

Jays players were surprised because they had never witnessed anything like this before in Toronto. "The people have always acted real civil here," said veteran designated hitter Cliff Johnson of the Blue Jays. "I was surprised. But who's to say those guys were real fans. Real fans would have been watching the game."

Toronto third baseman Garth Iorg was a little more blunt. "I wish I was a security guard," he said. "I could have gone out and nailed some of those suckers."

Toronto center fielder Lloyd Moseby was almost struck by a bottle thrown from the bleachers. "It was a total embarrassment," he said. "That wasn't the real Toronto."

The fans weren't the only ones to louse up Opening Day for the Blue Jays. The Orioles did their part, too, beating Toronto 2–1.

BATTY BATTERS

A hitter's greatest fear is not necessarily going 0-for-July or possessing an average that would embarrass a bowler. No, his worst fear is looking bad at the plate. Some of the game's best-known players have taken their turn at bat and returned to the dugout without a shred of dignity, leaving behind a residue of shame that even the garbageman won't touch. For "The Most Pitiful Hitting Performances," The Baseball Hall of SHAME inducts the following:

Tony Horton

First Baseman • Cleveland, A.L. • June 24, 1970

Tony Horton was so fooled on a pitch that he wound up literally *crawling* back to the dugout in shame.

In the ninth inning of a 7–2 Cleveland victory over the Yankees in New York, reliever Steve Hamilton was facing Horton. On occasion, Hamilton liked to toss a high-arching slow pitch that he fondly called his "folly floater." Three weeks earlier, he had thrown one to Horton in Cleveland and the first baseman singled. Afterward, Tony asked Hamilton if he would throw it again sometime because the slugger was sure he could clobber the bizarre pitch for a homer.

So when Horton stepped into the batter's box against Hamilton at Yankee Stadium, he asked for the "floater." The hurler nodded. The tantalizing slow ball crossed the plate, but Tony was too eager and he fouled it off. The likable Horton begged for a second chance and Hamilton, being an accommodating fellow, tossed another tempting slow ball. "I never thought he'd throw two in a row," Tony recalled. The powerfully built home run hitter took a mighty cut but all he could do was foul out weakly to the catcher.

Horton was so mortified that he threw his cap and bat into the air. Then to the shock and amusement of fans and players alike, Tony dropped to his

NYT Pictures

knees and crawled back to the dugout on all fours. Everyone erupted in laughter—even his own manager, Alvin Dark.

The fans cheered with delight, causing Hamilton to remark after the game, "That's the biggest ovation I ever got in fourteen years as a pro athlete."

Minnie Minoso

Outfielder • Cleveland, A.L. • July 17, 1959

The most pitiful thing that can happen to a batter is to be called out on strikes. However, Minnie Minoso found an even more ignoble way to disgrace himself at the plate. He managed to get called out on strikes without ever setting foot in the batter's box.

Minoso's moment of infamy came during a heated rhubarb at Fenway Park in the eighth inning of a game between the Cleveland Indians and the Boston Red Sox. Trouble brewed when Cleveland manager Joe Gordon vehemently protested an interference call on an Indians base runner. Failing to change the mind of the second base umpire, Gordon took up his battle with plate umpire Frank Umont.

Gordon's bellyaching got him nowhere—except booted out of the game. Furious over the ejection, Gordon ran over to his third base coach, Jo-Jo White, and told him what to say to Umont. White tried, but the umpire was in no mood for further discussion and ordered Minoso, the next batter, to step up to the plate.

But since the Indians were still in an uproar and continued to squawk at the arbiters, Minnie refused to budge from his spot near the on-deck circle. Again, Umont motioned for Minoso to get into the batter's box. Again, Minnie stayed put about a dozen feet from the plate.

Umont wasn't about to put up with any more grandstanding by Minoso, so the ump ordered Bosox hurler Leo Kiely to pitch to an empty batter's box. Kiely delivered three straight strikes and Umont declared Minnie out.

Only then did Minoso spring into action. First, he hurled his bat at the umpire's feet. Then he charged after Umont as though he were going to tear him to pieces. It took a platoon of umpires and players to restrain the infuriated player. Teammate Rocky Colavito literally dragged him away.

Minoso was not only called out, he was thumbed out, too.

"LaLob" Victim No. 1: Gorman Thomas
Outfielder • Milwaukee, A.L. • September 10, 1981

"LaLob" Victim No. 2: Lamar Johnson
Pinch Hitter • Texas, A.L. • August 6, 1982

No two batters looked sillier striking out in a plate appearance than Gorman Thomas and Lamar Johnson.

The sluggers became the humiliated victims of "LaLob," the descendant of the old blooper pitch introduced by Rip Sewell of the Pirates in the 1940s. "LaLob," a high-arching, lazy change of pace that had hitters swinging from their heels, was a favorite pitch of Yankees reliever Dave LaRoche. It was once clocked at a blazing 28 mph, reportedly the slowest time ever recorded for a pitched ball.

The secret to hitting the pitch was timing, and during a game at Yankee Stadium, Thomas failed miserably. With Milwaukee Brewers at second and third and two out in the top of the sixth inning, Gorman stepped in against LaRoche. Thomas took the first "LaLob" for a ball and then fouled off the second one. "He's going to throw me another one, isn't he?" Gorman asked Yankees catcher Barry Foote. The catcher just laughed. Sure enough, LaRoche threw a third straight "LaLob" and this time Thomas tried to bunt it, but the ball rolled foul. Having two strikes on Gorman, LaRoche tried to fool him by throwing a fastball. But the pitch was called a ball. So LaRoche returned with "LaLob." Thomas swung with enough force to spawn a tornado—and missed. Gorman was so exasperated and embarrassed that he flung his batting helmet up in the air and then, before it hit the ground, shattered it with his bat.

It was a tough night for Thomas. When he came out to take the field at the end of the inning, he tripped over the dugout steps.

Remembering how embarrassed Gorman was by "LaLob," LaRoche decided to give him another chance the next time the two faced each other. A year later, on June 30, 1982, the Yankees were trailing 6–1 in the fifth inning when Thomas stepped into the batter's box against LaRoche. "I felt I owed him one at-bat because of what happened the previous year," the pitcher recalled. "I shook my head at him as if to say, 'I'm going to keep throwing it until you do something with it.'"

So LaRoche threw Thomas seven straight "LaLobs." Gorman took one for a ball and fouled off five pitches before lining the last one to left field for a single. When Thomas reached first, LaRoche smiled and tipped his hat to him. Gorman smiled back—and then stuck his tongue out.

Lamar Johnson's plate appearance against LaRoche was even screwier. On August 6, 1982, Johnson was called on to pinch-hit for the Texas Rangers, who were losing to the Yankees 6–0 with two out in the ninth inning.

Flinging conventional pitches, LaRoche got two quick strikes on Lamar. Then the pitcher served up his patented "LaLob." Johnson took a mighty Casey-at-the-Bat swing and whiffed—screwing himself into a heap on the ground. As Lamar lay there giggling helplessly, home plate umpire Ken Kaiser counted him out like a referee over a fallen boxer. Then Kaiser helped Johnson to his feet as the players from both dugouts and the fans in the stands roared with delight.

"Ordinarily, I'm not too fond of 'LaLob,'" said Yankees manager Clyde King. "But I couldn't help but break up when Johnson was lying on the plate. What a batting performance!" A batty performance was more like it.

Richie Ashburn

Outfielder • Philadelphia, N.L. • August 17, 1957

It wasn't enough that Richie Ashburn hit a screaming foul into the stands that smacked a grandmother in the face. No, as the injured fan was being carried out on a stretcher, Ashburn whacked another foul that struck the *same* poor fan again!

"I didn't mean to do it," Ashburn said when told that this deplorable batting performance was being inducted into *The Baseball Hall of SHAME 3*. "When I saw what happened, I felt terrible."

Not as terrible as Alice Roth, who had taken her two grandsons to see the New York Giants play the Philadelphia Phillies at Connie Mack Stadium. "We were sitting behind third base and Richie was fouling off a lot of balls," recalled her grandson Preston, who was eight years old at the time. "My grandmother was fixing my cap and never saw the ball coming. It hit her square in the face."

The blow broke Mrs. Roth's nose and left her dazed and bleeding.

Medical personnel immediately rushed to her aid and placed her on a stretcher. Preston suffered a blow of sorts, too. Although he and his brother Tom were upset, Preston had the presence of mind to notice that a man sitting in front of them had ended up with the ball. Preston recalled, "I asked him if I could have the ball. He just looked at me and said, 'Go to hell, kid.' "

Mrs. Roth's ordeal wasn't over yet. Play on the field had halted momentarily while the teams focused their attention on the injured woman. When Mrs. Roth was placed on a stretcher, play resumed and Ashburn stepped back into the batter's box. Too bad the medical personnel didn't take her out just a little bit quicker. While Mrs. Roth was being carried off on the stretcher, Ashburn swatted another wicked foul that struck the helpless woman again!

If Ashburn had to hit someone with a batted ball, he could have done better. Mrs. Roth was the wife of Earl Roth, sports editor of the *Philadelphia Bulletin*.

Ashburn felt so bad about the incident that he visited her regularly in the hospital and brought her bouquets. The team gave her grandsons free tickets and a tour of the clubhouse, where they met the players and received an autographed baseball. Apparently, the boys forgot the painful reason for the red carpet treatment. Recalled their mother, Mrs. Dorothy Roth, "For my two sons, this was quite exciting. When it was all over and poor Grandma was still suffering in the hospital, the boys went to visit her. One of them asked her, 'Grandma, do you think you could go to an Eagles game and get hit in the face with a football?' "

RUN FOR YOUR LIVES!

Some players are such horrendous runners they could use a second base coach. It's not that their legs are slow as much as it is that their minds are working at only quarter speed. To others, running the base paths can be as foolish and reckless as strolling down a dark alley at midnight. For "The Most Absurd Baserunning Fiascoes," The Baseball Hall of SHAME inducts the following:

Rickey Henderson

Outfielder • Oakland, A.L. • July 25, 1982

Record-setting base stealer Rickey Henderson is one of the game's most daring and exciting players. Yet he is the same base runner who once was called out while advancing from first to third on a ground-rule double!

As you know, anyone—even your kid sister—can safely stroll from first to third on a ground-rule double. But Rickey found an embarrassing way to mess up the easiest baserunning task in baseball.

In the top of the fifth inning in a game against the Orioles in Baltimore, Henderson was on first base with Dwayne Murphy at the plate. On the pitch to Murphy, Rickey took off for second and slid into the base headfirst before realizing that Murphy had looped an opposite-field fly ball to left.

When Henderson saw that Murphy's ball might be caught, he got up and began to retreat toward first. But Murphy's ball landed safely and then bounced into the seats for a ground-rule double. So Henderson headed across the infield to third. But he witlessly forgot to retouch second base.

Orioles second baseman Rich Dauer spotted the infraction and called for the ball at second. When pitcher Dennis Martinez tossed the ball to Dauer, umpire Nick Bremigan called Henderson out.

A's manager Billy Martin rushed out of the dugout to argue. He wasn't about to buy Bremigan's citation of the rule which says that a runner must retouch a base once he relinquishes it. Martin claimed the ball was dead once it was ruled a ground-rule double. He lost his case. And Rickey lost a run for Oakland. Dan Meyer followed the controversial play with a two-run homer—a blast that would have been a game-tying three-run shot if Henderson hadn't goofed up. Several Oakland players waved towels from the dugout and heckled Bremigan after Meyer's homer. The A's should have directed their anger at one of their own—Rickey Henderson, who seemed to forget that, in baseball, the shortest route between two points is not a straight line.

Gates Brown

Pinch Hitter • Detroit, A.L. • August 7, 1968

Gates Brown gave the most disgraceful exhibition of hot-dogging on the base paths that the game has ever seen.

Before a home game against the Cleveland Indians, Detroit Tigers manager Mayo Smith decided that rather than start Brown, he would use him as a pinch hitter if the situation warranted it.

In the sixth inning, with Cleveland leading 2–1, Gates, a 220-pound player whose love for baseball was exceeded only by his love for food, sneaked out of the dugout and into the clubhouse for a snack. Brown grabbed two hot dogs, slapped some mustard and ketchup on them, and hustled back to the dugout.

Sitting in the far corner, he planned on eating the hot dogs on the sly. He also figured he had plenty of time to munch on them because Smith almost never called on Gates to pinch-hit until late in the game. Brown had just taken a bite out of his first hot dog when, from the other end of the dugout, he heard Smith say, "Gates, get your bat and hit."

Brown was not prepared to play. His belt was unbuckled, his shoes were untied, and he was holding a hot dog in each hand. By turning his back to Smith, Gates was able to hide his dilemma from the manager. But since Smith was still staring at him, Brown couldn't dump the hot dogs without getting into trouble. So Gates stuffed the doggies in his jersey, tied his shoes, fastened his belt, grabbed a bat, and headed for the batter's box.

"I always wanted to get a hit every time I went up to the plate," recalled Brown. "But this was one time I didn't want to get a hit. I'll be damned if I didn't smack one in the gap and I had to slide into second—headfirst, no less. I was safe with a double. But when I stood up, I had mustard and ketchup and smashed hot dogs and buns all over me.

"The fielders took one look at me, turned their backs, and damned near busted a gut laughing at me. My teammates in the dugout went crazy. That had to be my most embarrassing moment in baseball."

Brown's hit helped win the game, but, he confessed, "I was still pissed off because I messed up my hot dogs and I couldn't eat them."

Although his uniform was stained with mustard and ketchup, Gates had plenty of Mayo with his hot dogs. The manager fined him $100. "When I returned to the dugout," Brown recalled, "Smith said, 'What the hell were you doing eating on the bench in the first place?' I decided to tell him the truth. I said, 'I was hungry. Besides, where else can you eat a hot dog and have the best seat in the house?' "

Frank Robinson   Russ Snyder

Outfielder   **Outfielder**
Baltimore, A.L. • August 11, 1967

On rare occasions, a boneheaded runner will pass another teammate on the base path for an automatic out. But not the way Frank Robinson and Russ Snyder did it. They passed each other while running in opposite directions!

In a game against the Detroit Tigers, the visiting Baltimore Orioles were batting in the third inning when Snyder lined a one-out single. Robinson then drilled a shot over 400 feet to deep center field, driving outfielder Jim Northrup to the wall. Northrup leaped for the ball, but it popped out of his glove when he banged into the fence.

Robinson, figuring he had a sure double, roared around first and headed for second. But Snyder, who had already reached second, wrongly thought the ball had been caught. So he turned around and retreated as fast as he could toward first base. Somewhere between the two bases, the pair whizzed past each other. That was a no-no.

If Robinson had been more alert, he could have stopped Snyder before it was too late. If Snyder had been more alert, he could have been on third and Robby on second. Although Snyder was really to blame for the goof, umpire Jerry Neudecker had no choice but to call Robinson out for passing Snyder.

Jim Rice

Outfielder • Boston, A.L. • July 26, 1986

Slugging outfielder Jim Rice proved with embarrassing ease that he's paid millions of dollars for his hitting, not for his baserunning.

During a weekend series against the California Angels at Anaheim Stadium, the performance of the Bosox superstar between first and second was way off base. Twice he joined teammates in plays that belonged in an instructional video on how *not* to run the bases.

With one out in the top of the fourth inning, Rice singled, moving runner Bill Buckner to third. The next batter, Don Baylor, hit a fly to short center that was caught and then dropped by California's Gary Pettis. It turned out to be a lucky break—for the Angels.

Buckner planned to tag up at third and fake a run toward home just to draw a throw. But after seeing the muff, he broke for the plate. However, Pettis threw a strike to catcher Bob Boone, who tagged out the sliding Buckner at home.

While all this action was taking place, Rice was daydreaming off first base. He had turned his back on the play a split second before Pettis had dropped the ball. When Rice finally turned around, he saw Boone tag Buckner and then watched lamely as the catcher tossed the ball to second for the easy force-out.

Buckner shouldn't have run but did; Rice should have run but didn't. The result was a rally-killing double play in a game the Red Sox lost, 4–1.

The next day, Rice attempted an encore performance with the help of Wade Boggs. With Boggs on second, Rice on first, and one out in the eighth inning, California's Donnie Moore threw a pitch that bounced off Boone's glove to the right of home plate. It wasn't far enough away for Rice to take off. However, even though he's not known as a speed merchant, averaging only five steals a year, Rice broke for second anyway. This surprised everyone, including Boggs—who hadn't planned on leaving second. Forced off his perch, Boggs—who steals bases with even less frequency than Rice—lumbered toward third. Meanwhile, Rice reconsidered his hasty decision and retreated toward first. He made it back safely, but poor Boggs was nailed at third. Boston went on to lose, 3–0.

What made both these Rice-inspired goofs so ironic was that the Boston front office had hired former major leaguer Al Bumbry during the Red Sox's West Coast trip to help the team with its baserunning. After watching in horror at Rice's lack of base-path skills on the rare double play and the confusion the next day, Bumbry told reporters, "Hey, I can't run for him."

Earl Williams

Catcher • Atlanta-Montreal, N.L.; Baltimore-Oakland, A.L.
1970–77

Maury Wills, the great base stealer, once said, "It's just as important to know when not to go as it is to know when to go." Earl Williams knew when not to go.

No player ever went longer without stealing his very first base than the 6-foot, 3-inch, 215-pound catcher. Williams had nearly 3,000 at-bats before swiping a base.

Earl made no bones about his speed. "There's not much to say about speed when you don't have any," he once said. In spring training, the coaches didn't need a stopwatch to time his running—they needed a calendar. It took him so long to run the bases after a homer, the umpires threatened to eject him for delaying the game.

Ever since he broke into the majors in 1970, Williams had been chipping away at the all-time record for not stealing bases, which was held by another catcher, the much-traveled Russ Nixon. In his twelve-year career between 1957 and 1968, Nixon had 2,504 at-bats without stealing a single base.

That ignoble mark stood until July 13, 1976. On that steamy night, Earl made his 2,505th official plate appearance without having stolen a base. Afterward, in the Atlanta clubhouse, Williams was informed that he had broken an all-time major league record. He responded like a true champion. "What record?" he asked, scratching his head. "Most times grounding out to shortstop?" Once he learned the details, he shouted, "All right! I knew there was a reason why I never stole!"

Nixon, who was a Cincinnati Reds coach at the time, went into a mild state of shock when told that his mark had been eclipsed. That was because he had no idea he was a world-record holder in anything. All he could say was, "Holy cow!"

What makes the nonstealing feat all the more astounding is that the at-bat figures do not include the number of times Williams reached base on a walk, sacrifice, or hit by pitch. Apparently the pressure to go through an entire career with nearly 3,000 at-bats without a steal was too much to bear. In 1977, his final year in the bigs, Earl stole two bases.

Williams offered this advice to young players setting out to break his record: "You gotta work on getting a bad jump."

Lee Lacy

Outfielder • Pittsburgh, N.L. • July 24, 1979

Lee Lacy was a runner on first when the next batter walked. Yet incredibly, Lacy managed to get thrown out at second base! That's because he didn't keep his eyes and ears open.

In the bottom of the fourth inning, the visiting Cincinnati Reds were beating the Pittsburgh Pirates 4–3. But the Pirates were threatening with runners on first and third, two out, and batter Omar Moreno at the plate with a 3–1 count.

When Reds pitcher Fred Norman delivered the next pitch, Lacy broke from first base in an attempted steal. The pitch was called ball four by plate umpire Dave Pallone but catcher Johnny Bench instinctively fired the ball to shortstop Dave Concepcion. Lacy was called out at second by umpire Dick Stello. In reality, Lacy was safe because Moreno, who stood in the batter's box watching the play, had walked.

But Lacy didn't bother to check the call of the home plate umpire. Thinking he had been thrown out, Lacy left the bag at second and began trotting toward the dugout. However, when he saw Moreno start to move toward first base, he tried to scramble back to second base. But Concepcion made the tag—again. And Stello called him out—again.

The play triggered one of the longest arguments in decades. Lacy claimed Stello misled him when the ump called him out on the attempted steal. The umps eventually ruled that since Moreno had walked, Lacy initially was safe at second rather than caught stealing. But they also ruled he was out when he was subsequently tagged by Concepcion. When the argument ended thirty-four minutes later, Pittsburgh manager Chuck Tanner announced he was playing the game (won by the Reds 6–5) under protest.

The Pirates' protest was turned down by National League President Chub Feeney, who said, "Lacy left second base of his own volition and should have been aware of the possibilities of Moreno receiving a base on balls."

Bizarre happenings are nothing new to Lacy. Five years earlier, when he played for the Los Angeles Dodgers, he and several other players acted as if they were following a script from "Amazing Stories."

In a game against the Pirates, the Dodgers had the bases loaded and a 3–2 count on batter Joe Ferguson. Lacy, who was on third, thought the next pitch was a strike, so he headed for the dugout. Pirate catcher Manny Sanguillen assumed it was a strike, too, and rolled the ball toward the mound. But Jim Wynn, who was on second, thought Ferguson had walked and raced all the way home. Seeing Wynn run, Lacy changed his mind and followed suit. Chaos erupted. When players, managers, and umpires settled down, the verdict was that Ferguson had walked. Wynn was declared out for passing Lacy, but Lacy was safe at home.

HOLEY MITTS!

◆

You can tell who they are in the box score by their first initial: E. They are the fabulous fumblers who somehow make it to the bigs with holes in their gloves. These fielders have only one weakness— batted balls. They boot so many balls they belong on a soccer field, not a baseball diamond. For "The Most Inept Fielding Performances," The Baseball Hall of SHAME inducts the following:

Pepper Martin

Outfielder–Third Baseman • St. Louis, N.L. • 1928–44

When Pepper Martin played third base, he uncorked some of the wildest throws ever—on purpose. Rather than throw out the runner at first base, Martin sometimes deliberately tried to knock out the runner by firing the ball at his head.

Martin, whose ferocious style of play earned him the nickname "The Wild Horse of the Osage," simply hated to field bunts. Pegging beanballs at bunters was his not-so-subtle way of discouraging them from laying one down.

Before a game against the Braves in Boston in 1938, Cardinals manager Frankie Frisch announced that he would play Martin at third base, much to Pepper's dismay. So during batting practice, Martin walked over to Braves skipper Casey Stengel and warned, "You better tell your guys not to bunt on me, because if they do, I'm gonna soak [hit] 'em."

Naturally, Casey ordered his players to bunt toward third every chance they got. Pepper was so mad that when he charged in and picked up the ball, he zinged it right at the runner's head. Only the great leaping ability of first baseman Johnny Mize saved Martin from racking up a string of throwing errors.

"I couldn't believe it when I saw it," recalled Martin's teammate Terry

Moore. "The guys who tried to bunt on him had to keep one eye on Pepper and one eye on first base because they were worried about getting beaned in the back of the head."

By the time Braves first baseman Elbie Fletcher stepped to the plate, Martin was steaming. With little thought for his own welfare, Fletcher dropped a bunt down the third-base line. But when he saw what a terrific jump Martin got on the ball, Fletcher decided to run to the dugout rather than to first. Fletcher ducked his head down and cut away from the base line just as Martin wound up and fired a bullet over the button of Fletcher's cap. The ball smacked into the dugout and cleared the bench. Fletcher was awarded second base on Martin's overthrow but neither he nor any other Brave dared to bunt against Pepper again that day.

Larry Biittner

Outfielder • Chicago, N.L. • September 26, 1979

A "hat trick" spurs accolades in hockey, but Larry Biittner found out it triggers embarrassment in baseball.

Biittner was playing right field for the Chicago Cubs in an 8–3 loss to the New York Mets in Wrigley Field when Bruce Boisclair hit a sinking liner toward him. Biittner charged in and made a spectacular lunging dive at the hard-hit ball. Unfortunately, he trapped it. Then he scrambled to his feet so quickly his cap flew off. Biittner knew the only way to hold the runner to a single was to fire the ball in to second base in a hurry. There was only one problem. The ball wasn't in his glove and he couldn't find it anywhere.

Launching a frantic search, Biittner checked the warning track behind him, peered at the right-field bullpen, glanced at his helpless teammate in center field, and then looked toward the infield. No ball. Out of sheer frustration, Biittner even scanned the sky to see if a nasty pigeon had swooped down, snatched the ball, and carried it away.

Finally the perplexed outfielder picked up his hat in disgust. To his utter amazement, he found the ball. It was hidden under his cap the whole time!

By now, Boisclair was streaking for third base while the spectators and players were cracking up with laughter. Somehow Biittner managed to overcome his chagrin and throw out the Met runner.

After the game, Biittner was asked when he knew the ball was hidden under his hat. He replied, "When I couldn't find it anywhere else."

Tommy "Buckshot" Brown

Infielder • Brooklyn-Philadelphia-Chicago, N.L. • 1944–53

Buckshot Brown was an infielder with only one weakness—he couldn't throw the ball to first base.

While most infielders are blessed with rifle arms that fire balls with pinpoint accuracy, Brown was cursed with a shotgun arm that scattered throws everywhere, thus earning him the moniker "Buckshot."

Brown's errant tosses weren't your everyday, run-of-the-mill miscues. His were eye-popping, wild heaves that traveled far enough to be subject to the regulations of interstate commerce.

When Buckshot played shortstop for the Brooklyn Dodgers, his arm was considered so dangerous that the Ebbets Field grounds crew used to move the batting cage in front of the first-base boxes to protect the fans during infield practice. Whenever a ball was batted in his direction during a game, the fans behind first base instinctively ducked behind the seats because Brown's throw was an odds-on favorite to conk someone on the noggin.

"Everybody who sat behind first base sure stayed alert when Tommy was playing," recalled Ed Stevens, a Dodger first baseman who had the unenviable task of trying to snare Buckshot's haphazard pegs. "He'd throw balls six, seven, even ten rows up in the stands. Most of the time I didn't even try leaping for them because they were so high. I'd just stand there and watch them go. The best I could hope for was that the throws would hit the railing and bounce back. But they never did.

"His throws zinged toward first like a shotgun. They used to drive [Dodgers manager] Leo Durocher crazy. He'd scream and cuss at Tommy, but it didn't do any good."

Only sixteen when he joined the club in 1944, Buckshot distinguished himself by recording the lowest fielding percentage in the league that year—.925—averaging one error every three games. He "improved" on that ignoble mark the following season, with a woeful .918 fielding percentage, chalking up one error every 2.4 games.

No matter who the Dodgers put at first base, Buckshot could overthrow him—even 6-foot, 6-inch Howie "Stretch" Schultz. "Tommy threw them over my head without even trying," said Schultz, who still marvels at Brown's greatest tape-measure toss.

In a game against Boston at old Braves Field, Buckshot fielded a grounder and then uncorked a wild throw that ended way up in the thirtieth row. "You should have heard the Boston crowd," said Schultz. "They gave Buckshot a rousing cheer. They had never seen a throw head into outer space before."

Dave Winfield

Outfielder • San Diego, N.L. • April 30, 1974

Dave Winfield uncorked the most embarrassing throw ever made from the outfield.

He was one of several San Diego Padre outfielders who were having problems throwing the ball on target to the cutoff man, so manager John McNamara ordered them to work on their pegs before a game against the visiting Montreal Expos. During the special practice, all of Dave's throws were high and way off the mark. An exasperated McNamara kept yelling at him, "Hit the cutoff man! Hit the cutoff man!"

Later, during the game, Winfield had an opportunity to show his manager that he could indeed hit the cutoff man. The Expos had a runner on second base when the batter drilled a single to center field. Dave charged the ball, scooped it up cleanly, and prepared to gun down the runner at home plate.

Second baseman Derrel Thomas was lined up between Winfield and home to act as the cutoff man. But because the play didn't require a relay, he turned his back on Dave and crouched way down, almost to the ground, so he wouldn't be in the way of Winfield's throw. Thomas should have dug a trench.

With his strong arm, Dave flung a bullet toward home—and hit Thomas right in the butt! Thomas rolled around on the grass for a few minutes, holding his sore rear end while the players and fans roared with laughter.

"Well," said a chagrined Winfield after the game, "I finally hit the cutoff man."

George "Bingo" Binks

Outfielder • Washington-Philadelphia-St. Louis, A.L. • 1944–48

As an outfielder, Bingo Binks could do it all—he rambled far out of position, collided regularly with his teammates, threw to the wrong base, and sometimes didn't bother to throw the ball at all.

Oh yes, he also turned his manager's hair prematurely gray. That's because he could field but he just couldn't think. "Binks has the greatest glove I've ever seen on an outfielder but I can't use him as my regular starter," said Ossie Bluege, skipper of the Washington Senators. "I never can tell what he's going to do, because he doesn't know himself."

There was the day against the Boston Red Sox in 1945 when, with one out and a man on second, Bingo galloped into deep center field to make a spectacular one-handed catch of Bob Johnson's long fly. Binks was so proud of his fielding feat that he strutted around like a peacock. But he ended up looking like a birdbrain—he forgot to throw the ball back to the infield! The runner tagged up and scored all the way from second base.

That same year, Bingo showed he could throw the ball when he had to, but too often his tosses weren't anywhere near the intended base. Once, while playing right field, he misjudged a fly ball for a moment, but then made a splendid recovery and caught the ball at his shoetops. However, Binks was so critical of himself that he promptly took the ball out of his glove and flung it to the ground in disgust. Unfortunately, he threw the ball down so quickly after catching it that the umpire ruled Binks never had possession and the batter wound up at second.

Bingo hurt his teammates in other ways, too. While playing center field, he collided into left fielder George Case so many times that Case convinced manager Bluege to shift Binks to right for the safety of both players. After that, there weren't any more collisions—because whoever played center field backed off and let Binks take any ball he could reach.

When Bingo played, Bluege stood on the dugout steps frantically trying to wave his wayward outfielder into position for the different hitters. Complained the manager, "I move him over to the left or the right as the case may be, and then between pitches Binks starts strolling around out there with his head down, and is back where he shouldn't be playing. I've always been afraid he's gonna walk out of the park someday."

George Brace Photo

Although fans, players, and management laughed off most of Bingo's goof-ups, no one could overlook the worst blunder he ever made—it cost his team the American League pennant in 1945. It happened in Washington's final game of the season. A victory would have put the Senators into a first-place tie with the Detroit Tigers.

Playing against the Athletics in Philadelphia, the Senators were in a 3–3 deadlock in the bottom of the 12th inning. With two outs and nobody on base, A's batter Ernie Kish sent a high fly toward Binks for what appeared to be a routine catch. But as the ball descended, Binks covered up like a battered fighter going into a defensive shell. Bingo had forgotten to put on his sunglasses and he lost the ball in the glare. The ball dropped safely for a cheap double and, moments later, George Kell won the game with a run-scoring single.

It was as dead and still as a morgue in the Senators' dressing room after the game. Dumbfounded after their critical 4–3 defeat, the players stole angry glances at the sorrowful Bingo, but said nothing. Less pitiless, pitcher Mickey Haefner looked sourly at Binks and, breaking the silence, muttered, "They ought to fine you $4,000." He was talking of the potential World Series share each player would have received.

Binks didn't reply. Only a few minutes before his boner, when the Senators were at bat, A's center fielder Sam Chapman stopped the game with two out and went to the bench to get his sunglasses. Talk about a perfect warning for Bingo. But, alas, he chose to ignore it. Detroit copped the pennant, winning one more game than Washington.

After watching Binks play, baseball wizard Casey Stengel summed up Bingo's fielding style this way: "I can read the temper of friends, the whims of women, and the changes of weather. But I cannot predict what George Binks will be up to next. He is baseball's magnificent unpredictable."

Dutch Leonard

Pitcher • Washington, A.L. • August 1, 1945

It's one thing to lose the ball in the sun. It's quite another to lose the ball in your pants.

Washington Senators pitcher Dutch Leonard was robbed of a fielding assist by his baggy pantaloons, causing him to curse the sons of britches.

Leonard was hurling a two-hit shutout against the visiting Philadelphia Athletics in the eighth inning when A's batter Irvin Hall lined a knuckleball right back to the mound. The ball smacked into Dutch's stomach and he doubled over, holding his glove in front of his belt. Leonard, who wasn't hurt, thought he had trapped the ball between his belly and his mitt. But when he straightened up to throw Hall out at first, Dutch was shocked to

discover the ball was not in his glove. Frantically, he searched the mound and the infield. Nothing.

Where could it be? Suddenly, Leonard felt something weird inside his pants. It was the ball! Somehow, when he doubled over, the ball rolled down his shirt, through his loosely belted waist, and into his left pant leg. By the time Dutch removed the ball from his pants, Hall was already perched on first, laughing hysterically along with the rest of the players and the crowd.

From then on, Leonard buckled his belt a notch tighter.

Lennie Merullo

Shortstop • Chicago, N.L. • September 13, 1942

No infielder ever played a more shameful inning than Lennie Merullo.

He turned shortstop into a disaster area during the second inning of a game against the Boston Braves at Braves Field. Every time Lennie touched the ball, he booted it—on four consecutive plays.

It all started when Clyde Kluttz tapped an easy grounder to Merullo, who muffed it for error No. 1. Ducky Detweiler then stroked a single to right field as Kluttz raced to third. When Detweiler broke for second base on the throw-in by outfielder Bill Nicholson, Lennie attempted to cut off the peg, but dropped the ball for error No. 2. That put runners on second and third.

After the next batter struck out, Tommy Holmes sent another grounder to Merullo who once again bobbled the ball for error No. 3 as Kluttz scored. An ignoble record was within Lennie's grasp, even if the balls hit to him in the inning weren't.

Sure enough, Al Roberge then dinked a roller to the Cubs' fumble-fingered shortstop. This time, Merullo gloved the ball without mishap, but just as he started to throw to second for a force-out, the ball squirted out of his hand and bounced off his head. The fourth and record-setting error was his.

However, if ever a player had an excuse for screwing up this badly, it was Merullo. Just hours earlier, he had become the proud and nervous father of his first child, a seven-pound, four-ounce son. After the game, the baby was given a new nickname in honor of this unforgettable day: Boots.

EVERY TRICK IN
THE BOOK

◆

To be a major leaguer, you need to learn the fundamentals of the game: laying down a bunt, running the bases, and making the pivot on a double play. But to gain that extra edge that could mean the difference between winning and losing, players need to master the finer points: how to doctor a ball, load up a bat, or use devious methods to psych out the opponent. For "The Sneakiest Chicanery Perpetrated by Players," The Baseball Hall of SHAME inducts the following:

Bob Moose

Pitcher • Pittsburgh, N.L. • August 29, 1968

Remember back in 1983 when George Brett caused such a shameful ruckus over his infamous pine-tar bat? Well, fifteen years earlier, Pittsburgh Pirates pitcher Bob Moose also got in trouble using the sticky stuff—for throwing a pine-tar *ball.*

Moose, then a twenty-year-old rookie, didn't bother with the tried-and-true spitter or Vaseline ball. No, he was an innovator. He discovered the pitch out of necessity. Working against the league-leading St. Louis Cardinals, Moose was roughed up for two runs and four hits in the first inning. In the bottom of the inning, Moose was watching a teammate in the on-deck circle rubbing pine tar on his bat. Suddenly it dawned on Moose that the black goo might do wonders on a ball. So he rubbed his pitching hand with pine tar and went out to the mound for the second inning.

Moose looked like Cy Young as his ball dipped and dived. The batters couldn't hit him. However, when Moose struck out four Cardinals in a row,

St. Louis manager Red Schoendienst became suspicious. He called time and demanded that plate umpire Chris Pelekoudas inspect the hurler's hand. Sure enough, the ump found enough pine tar to make George Brett proud.

"Why, Moose had so much pine tar on his right hand, his fingers stuck together," claimed Schoendienst. "Pelekoudas threw a new ball to Moose once, and when Moose threw it to the batter, the ball looked like somebody had used a paintbrush on it."

Following the umpire's orders, Moose went into the clubhouse and washed off the pine tar. Then he returned to the mound where he promptly gave up two more hits and two more runs in the inning before he was yanked for a reliever.

After the game, won by St. Louis 5–0, Cardinals outfielder Curt Flood said of Moose's black hand, "Why, it looked just like mine."

Amos Otis

Outfielder • Kansas City, A.L.; New York–Pittsburgh, N.L. • 1967–84

One of baseball's unwritten rules is "Do anything you can get away with." Amos Otis followed that rule to the letter.

Otis, a star outfielder for the Kansas City Royals, recently revealed a secret known to only a handful of teammates—he used a loaded bat for the last fourteen years of his career.

"Baseball officials can't do anything about it now," said the five-time All-Star, "but my bats were loaded. I had enough cork and superballs in there to blow away anything." He said he used loaded bats as far back as 1970 when he first joined the Royals.

"I had a very close friend who made the bats for me," Otis admitted. "He'd drill a hole down the barrel and stuff some superballs and cork in it. Then he put some sawdust back into the hole, sandpapered it down, and added a little pine tar over the top of it. The bat looked brand new."

With the Otis swing, the mass of a thirty-five-ounce bat took on the whiplash quickness of a thirty-two-ouncer. A doctored bat with a lively corked center can add fifty feet to the distance the ball travels. "Over my whole career, it probably meant about 193 home runs for me," said Otis, who in his career hit exactly 193 homers.

"I had a lot of fun knowing that I had an illegal bat, but I don't suppose opposing pitchers will be too happy when they hear about this. I never mentioned the bats to too many people. There were only a couple of players on the team who knew about them, and they couldn't say anything."

Although players face fines and suspensions for using loaded bats, Otis said he was never punished, even though he was caught once. "Back in 1971, I hit a line drive into center field and the bat split right at home plate and cork went flying all over the place. [Home plate umpire] Nestor Chylak kicked it away because a runner was coming home on the play. The next time up, Chylak said, 'If you're going to load them, make sure you get rid of them.' He could have nailed me."

Now, only a few short years since the end of his playing days, Otis says he's thrilled to be honored for his hitting—and his cheating. On June 8, 1986, Otis was inducted into the Kansas City Royals' Hall of Fame, and in his opening remarks he said, "It's not every day you get inducted into a Hall of Fame—whether it's in Royals Stadium or Cooperstown—*and* the Hall of SHAME. I've gotten in two out of three."

Lenny Randle

Third Baseman • Seattle, A.L. • May 27, 1981

No third baseman ever blew a play more outrageously than Lenny Randle.

It happened in the top of the sixth inning in a game between the visiting Kansas City Royals and the Seattle Mariners. When K.C. batter Amos Otis topped a ball toward third, three Mariners converged on it, but they realized the roller was too slow for them to throw out Otis. All they could hope for was that the ball would turn foul.

The ball kept rolling straight, hugging the line in fair territory. Suddenly, Randle was struck with a brainstorm. He dropped down on all fours. Then he huffed and he puffed and he blew the ball foul.

Initially, plate umpire Larry McCoy signaled a foul ball. But after Royals manager Jim Frey protested, the call was changed to a hit. The umpires cited the rule book, which states that a player cannot alter the course of the baseball. Randle had done just that with his head's down play.

"I didn't blow on it," he told reporters after the game. "I used the power

of suggestion. I was just telling the ball, 'Go foul, go foul.' The Bird [Detroit pitcher Mark Fidrych] used to talk to the ball and he didn't get into any trouble. How could they call it a hit? It was a foul ball."

Mariners manager Rene Lachemann backed up his infielder. "Lenny's breath from his yelling must have moved it," he said with an impish smile.

The blown play was "one of the big moments in the history of the Kingdome," declared Seattle's public relations director Bob Porter. "We don't have any wind in our indoor stadium, but that night we had a breeze and it was created by Lenny Randle."

Pete Rose

Third Baseman • Cincinnati, N.L. • July 11, 1978

Pete Rose masterminded and pulled off a devious plot that deliberately psyched out the American League team before the start of the 1978 All-Star Game.

Even though the National League had won 6 straight and 14 out of the previous 15 games, Rose still was looking for that extra edge against the junior circuit's All-Stars. So he concocted a scheme to make the National League hitters look more powerful than they really were. He arranged for Mizumo, a Japanese sporting goods company, to ship him dozens of Japanese baseballs. Because they are made smaller and sewn tighter, they carry much farther than major league baseballs do.

"I brought the balls in for the National League's batting practice," Rose explained with a grin. "It was all for psychological warfare.

"There was all this talk going on—still is, for that matter—about how the American League couldn't do anything against the National League. Well, I was always looking for ways to take advantage of that, kind of get under their skin and remind them in subtle ways that they really weren't as good as us."

When Rose arranged to have the Japanese balls smuggled into San Diego Stadium, the rest of the National Leaguers went along with the conspiracy and agreed to use the balls in batting practice. Then Rose went over to the American League's clubhouse and conned many of the players into watching the National League's batting practice.

"Everyone was hitting them out of the park," recalled Larry Bowa, an All-Star second baseman for the Philadelphia Phillies at the time. "I even hit a couple out in BP—something I never did before. It made me feel like Babe Ruth blasting those babies out of there.

"I remember some of the American League players were watching our guys wallop those balls and they were just in awe with their mouths wide open.

"We thought it was funnier than hell. As soon as our BP was over, we made sure we gathered up all those balls and got them out of there. Then we sat around and watched the American League take their BP. They were just barely hitting them to the outfield wall. It was normal stuff, but after the way our balls were flying way up high into the stands, the American Leaguers looked like Little Leaguers."

The plot worked. The National League won for the seventh straight time, clubbing the American League, 7–3.

"We were having a great time beating the American League all the time and using those Japanese balls was just one more way to psych them out and rub their noses in it," said Bowa. "Leave it to Pete to come up with a new angle."

Tito Francona

First Baseman • Cleveland, A.L. • June 11, 1962

Tito Francona's sneakiness helped steal a victory when he proved the old adage "Rules are made to be broken."

In a scoreless game between the visiting Cleveland Indians and the Boston Red Sox, the Indians loaded the bases against pitcher Earl Wilson. As Wilson went into his windup, Francona, the runner on first, cupped his hands to his mouth and shouted, "Hold it, Earl! Hold it!" Figuring time had been called—after all, who would stoop that low to trick a pitcher?—Wilson held on to the ball. Unfortunately, time had never been called. By not following through on his pitching motion, Wilson stumbled off the mound and was called for a balk. The runner on third waltzed home with what proved to be the winning run as the other runners moved up a base.

Bosox manager Mike Higgins rushed from the dugout after the balk call and protested Francona's dastardly deed. Rule 4:06 (3) clearly states that "no player shall call time or employ any other word or phrase or commit any act while the ball is alive for the obvious purpose of trying to make the pitcher commit a balk." However, the umpires claimed they didn't hear anything and declined to enforce the rule.

After his manager lost the argument, Wilson was still stewing on the mound. Unable to concentrate on batter Willie Kirkland, Wilson threw him a fat pitch that Kirkland smashed into the Red Sox bullpen for a 4–0 lead.

When Francona faced Wilson two innings later, the fuming hurler tried to nail him with a fastball in the ribs, but Tito skirted out of the way. On the next pitch, Francona tapped a grounder toward first, and when Wilson ran over to cover the bag, he narrowly missed bowling Tito over.

After the game, the Red Sox complained bitterly about Francona's dirty trick. When the press asked him for a comment, Tito just smiled. This time he kept his mouth shut.

SWAP SLOP

General managers claim they make trades to better the team. But it's often the other team they make better. Baseball is blighted with execs who couldn't find talent at the All-Star Game. With their skills at dealing, these GMs would trade their Cadillac for a rusty Volkswagen and an Edsel to be named later. For "The Dumbest Trades Ever Made," The Baseball Hall of SHAME inducts the following:

Willie McGee for Bob Sykes

October 21, 1981

The St. Louis Cardinals made a pigeon out of New York Yankees owner George Steinbrenner.

When the Yankees signed Dave Winfield in 1981, Steinbrenner decided to dump twenty-three-year-old rookie outfielder Willie McGee. Since he saw absolutely no potential in McGee, Steinbrenner naturally was delighted when the Cardinals offered a swap—McGee for left-handed reliever Bob Sykes. Although Sykes sported a lackluster 12–13 record with St. Louis, Steinbrenner gloated over the trade. After all, he told his front office, he was giving up an unknown rookie for a veteran pitcher.

McGee didn't stay unknown for long. He batted .296 to help lead the Cardinals to the 1982 World Series. In the third game of the Series against the Milwaukee Brewers, McGee wowed the sports world by hitting two homers, preventing two Brewer homers with leaping catches, and causing Cardinals Manager Whitey Herzog to say, "Nobody ever played a better World Series game than Willie did." McGee's career soared to new heights in 1985 when he led the majors in hitting with a lofty .353 batting average and was named the National League's Most Valuable Player.

As for Sykes, he started the 1982 season in Triple A for the Yankees. He suffered an arm injury, finished the campaign in Double A, and disappeared from baseball.

Steinbrenner was so upset over his bum deal that after the Series he demanded Cardinals owner August Busch, Jr., provide him with additional compensation for his own stupid trading. Busch refused—until the conniving Steinbrenner tried a little extortion. The Yankee owner knew that Busch was leading an owners movement to fire baseball commissioner Bowie Kuhn. Steinbrenner said he would vote to retain Kuhn unless the Cards sweetened the sour trade they had made with the Yanks. On December 1, 1982, a majority of the owners—including Steinbrenner—voted to fire Kuhn. Two weeks later, St. Louis sent the Yankees Bobby Meacham and Stan Javier as additional compensation for McGee.

Lou Piniella for Lindy McDaniel

December 7, 1973

In keeping with the New York Yankee tradition of fleecing Kansas City of baseball talent, the Yanks traded aging relief pitcher Lindy McDaniel for one of the Royals' best hitters, Lou Piniella.

Although Sweet Lou batted .285 during his five years at Kansas City, the Royals thought so little of him that they shipped him to New York for thirty-eight-year-old McDaniel, who owned a 34–28 record with the Yankees.

Over the next eleven years, Piniella soared to stardom in pinstripes, hitting for an average of .294 and spurring New York to four World Series. Because of his deep emotional commitment to the game and his unswerving loyalty to the Yankees, Piniella became one of the team's most popular players—and eventually its manager.

As for Lindy McDaniel, he lasted just two years with the Royals and won only six games before fading from the baseball scene.

Manager Joe Gordon for Manager Jimmy Dykes

August 3, 1960

If ever there was an even trade, this was it—both sides lost.

In one of the daffiest trades ever, Cleveland Indians general manager Frank Lane and Detroit Tigers president Bill DeWitt decided to swap managers during the season! Joe Gordon went to sixth-place Detroit and Jimmy Dykes went to fourth-place Cleveland. So where did the teams wind up at the end of the year? Detroit, sixth; Cleveland, fourth. The two skippers had almost identical losing records. Gordon was 26–31 at Detroit while Dykes finished 26–32 at Cleveland.

AP/Wide World Photos

The deal was struck not to help the teams but to solve some vexing problems for both Lane and DeWitt. Lane was desperately eager to unload Gordon. He actually fired Gordon just days before the end of the 1959 season. But the Cleveland fans were enraged. They booed Lane when he walked through the stands and deluged the front office with letters of protest. Lane, who was collecting a nickel for each paid admission, was practical enough to realize he had made a miscalculation. So he had to swallow a large chunk of crow and rehire Gordon.

Nevertheless, Lane was still looking for a way to ease Gordon out of the picture. Meanwhile, DeWitt was racking his brain for some unobtrusive way of dumping Dykes, who just wasn't his kind of manager. The bizarre trade was the answer.

Incredibly, this wasn't the first time the two GMs had concluded an absurd transaction that year. To the outrage of fans throughout the Great Lakes, the two teams' star hitters had been traded for each other the day before the 1960 season opened, home run king Rocky Colavito moving to Detroit in exchange for batting champion Harvey Kuenn.

Is it any wonder that Bill DeWitt and Frank Lane were soon bounced from their jobs?

Ryne Sandberg and Larry Bowa for Ivan DeJesus

January 27, 1982

The Philadelphia front office was cheering. They had just obtained a much-needed veteran shortstop, Ivan DeJesus, from the Chicago Cubs. All they had to do was give up what they felt was an untested rookie, Ryne Sandberg, and an aging infielder, Larry Bowa. It didn't take long for the Philly cheers to turn to tears.

Sandberg, then twenty-three, quickly established himself as a rising star with his glove and bat. He spearheaded the Cubs' climb to respectability in the NL East. In 1984, his third year with the team, the slick-fielding, dangerous-hitting second baseman keyed the club to its first division title, was voted an All-Star, and was named the National League's Most Valuable Player. The Gold Glove second baseman also sparkled in the field, making only six errors that season, one more than the record low for his position.

Meanwhile, his double-play partner, shortstop Larry Bowa, provided much-needed leadership and experience as the Cubs moved from fifth place in 1982 to first in 1984.

In return, the Phillies got only three years' service out of DeJesus before he was traded to St. Louis. However, before he left, he did manage to get his name in the record book. In 1983, DeJesus tied a major league record for fewest double plays by a shortstop in a season (150 or more games) with 64. That same year, he set a National League mark for fewest chances accepted by a shortstop. Apparently, the Phillies didn't want to take any more chances with him either.

Steve Carlton for Rick Wise

February 25, 1972

St. Louis Cardinals owner August Busch, Jr., made this deal in a fit of pique. If he was mad then, he has even more reason to be angry today—at himself.

At the end of the 1971 season, left-handed hurler Steve Carlton presumably was an honored, esteemed member of the Cardinals, having won 20 games while losing only 9. He felt he deserved a raise and held out for more money. Nothing could have been more upsetting to his employer, who viewed Carlton's action as treason. Treason to the august Busch means questioning his reputation for treating employees with extreme fairness— from the owner's view, of course.

So Busch did what any self-respecting tightwad would have done—he banished Carlton from the second-place Cardinals to the worst team in baseball at the time, the Philadelphia Phillies. In exchange, St. Louis received right-hander Rick Wise, a 17-game winner for the lowly Phils.

All Carlton did the next season was go 27–10, tying Sandy Koufax's National League modern-day record for most wins by a lefty. Carlton ended up with a spectacular 1.97 ERA and whiffed 310 batters to pick up the first of his unprecedented four Cy Young Awards. For the rest of the 1970s and the early 1980s, Carlton, a 300-game winner, was the most dominant left-hander in the league, steering the Phillies to five division titles and a World Championship. He ranks among the top 20 in six all-time pitching categories.

Wise, meanwhile, recorded a 32–28 record with the Cardinals before being traded to Boston. He is best known for having the same name as a popular potato chip.

Keith Hernandez for Neil Allen and Rick Ownbey

June 15, 1983

When St. Louis Cardinals fans were informed during a home game that their All-Star first baseman Keith Hernandez had been traded to the New York Mets, they booed. They knew it was a dumb deal. Too bad the Cardinals' brass didn't know it, too.

Hernandez, who won the MVP award and batting crown in 1979, had garnered five straight Gold Gloves and spurred the Cardinals to the 1982 World Championship. So what did the front office think he was worth? Just two so-so pitchers, Neil Allen and Rick Ownbey.

Hernandez, one of the best-fielding first basemen today, carried a career batting average of .299 when he joined the Mets. Thanks in part to his hitting, slick glove, leadership, and All-Star seasons, the Mets climbed from the cellar in 1983 to the World Championship in 1986.

Meanwhile, in St. Louis, the fans' worst fears were realized in 1983. Without Hernandez, the world champs tumbled to fourth place, four games below the .500 mark.

Ownbey, who had a 1–3 record with a 4.67 ERA with the Mets, never did win a game for the Cardinals, failing in all four of his starts.

St. Louis had counted on Allen to bolster the bullpen. With New York in 1983, he had struggled with a 2–7 record and a 4.50 ERA. He even requested time off for what turned out to be "stress reaction." But although he wound up with a 20–16 mark over parts of three seasons with the Redbirds, Allen registered only eight saves during that time.

Perhaps Allen had a premonition about which team would come out on top in this deal. On the day of the swap, he told reporters, "I've been traded for somebody who is a somebody. They'll remember this trade years from now and they'll say, 'Who was Keith Hernandez traded for?'"

Jeff Reardon for Ellis Valentine

May 29, 1981

Montreal Expos outfielder Ellis Valentine was on the disabled list, had a puny batting average of .211, and was labeled a complainer by the front office.

"Perfect," said the New York Mets. "We'll take him." They wound up getting taken instead. They sent their right-handed relief ace Jeff Reardon north of the border in exchange for a lackluster player whose days were numbered.

Valentine, who upset the Expos when he refused to take batting practice on an auxiliary field in spring training, had been seeking a trade. When the deal was made, he told reporters, "I'll be happy to get away from this organization and into a new place."

It didn't take the Mets long to realize they'd be happy for Valentine to get away from *their* organization and into a new place. Limping into New York with a hamstring injury, he did little to lift the Mets out of the cellar. However, Valentine did have a Cy Young–type year in 1981—he batted .207 (three points lower than Young's career batting average).

Meanwhile, Reardon established himself as one of the top game-savers in baseball. An All-Star two years in a row, Reardon racked up a league-high 41 saves in 1985 and 35 saves in 1986.

The Johnnie LeMaster Trades

1985

Shortstop Johnnie LeMaster played for three different teams in 1985 and managed to make them all happy—when they dumped him.

It had something to do with his performance—or lack of it—at the plate and on the field. It also had something to do with his destiny. Johnnie LeMaster proved to be a jinx.

At the start of his eleventh season with the San Francisco Giants, LeMaster demanded to be traded. He was fed up with the Candlestick Park fans, who, in turn, were fed up with his weak stick and holey glove. Booed more often than the last six mayors of San Francisco combined, Johnnie wore a jersey one day with "BOO" on the back. He hoped it would cool things off. It didn't. The fans laughed once and then got back to their booing.

Even though he had yet to collect a hit in 1985 and possessed a lifetime batting average of only .226, LeMaster announced he was tired of playing for a losing team like San Francisco and wanted to be traded. The Giants granted his wish, sort of. Trying hard to contain their glee over finding a club desperate enough to want Johnnie, San Francisco traded him on May 7 to the lowly Cleveland Indians for two minor leaguers.

Cleveland manager Pat Corrales then issued a statement that he would soon regret: "LeMaster is my regular shortstop. Only Ozzie Smith is better defensively. Johnnie will solidify my defense." LeMaster responded to those nice words by committing six errors and hitting only .150 before he was benched after nine games. So Johnnie demanded to be traded—again.

On May 29, three weeks after he had arrived in Cleveland, LeMaster was dealt to the even-lowlier Pittsburgh Pirates for a minor league pitcher. The Indians were so anxious to pawn him off on the Pirates that the club even paid Johnnie a $100,000 "assignment fee" to go to Pittsburgh. "The whole thing was a collectively inspired mistake, so it required a collectively inspired remedy," said Cleveland general manager Peter Bavasi.

With the Pirates, LeMaster hit .155 in 22 games before he was released. For the year, he hit a pitiful .128 in his combined service with the three teams. What made the 1985 season so ironic for LeMaster—a player who was tired of being on a losing club—was that each team he played for finished last in its division that year.

Buzzy Wares for Stadium Rent

March 28, 1913

Buzzy Wares worked hard all spring trying to make the St. Louis Browns' roster. When the 5-foot, 10-inch, 150-pound infielder apparently survived all the cuts, he was thrilled. But his happiness was dashed by one of the most bizarre transactions in the annals of baseball.

The Browns used him as payment for their spring training stadium rent.

The players were packing for the trip back to St. Louis after six grueling weeks of training in Montgomery, Alabama, when Browns manager George Stovall asked Wares to step into his office. Buzzy thought that the skipper was going to compliment him on his fine performance during the spring. Meanwhile, Stovall was figuring out the best way to break some bad news to the rookie. The manager chose the direct approach: "Wares, I'm leaving you here in Montgomery."

"But why?" asked the devastated young player.

"You're the payment for our grounds rental." With that said, Stovall left the room.

Buzzy spent most of the season in Montgomery, playing minor league ball, according to the terms of the transaction. He was called up at the tail end of the season and played in 10 games for the Browns. Wares lasted only one more year in the majors.

TAKE ME OUT
TO THE BRAWL GAME

Many baseball players can hit, but few can fight. A typical fracas between teams looks like a 50-percent-off sale at Bloomingdale's— lots of shoving, a little scuffling, and some harsh words. But every now and then, the baseball field takes on the ugly specter of street-gang warfare. Players wield bats to bash heads, not baseballs, and they throw punches rather than pitches. For "The Most Flagrant Cases of Assault and Battery on the Field," The Baseball Hall of SHAME inducts the following:

Main Event: Lou Piniella vs. Carlton Fisk
Undercard: Graig Nettles vs. Bill Lee

New York • May 20, 1976

It was only May, but it might as well have been the Fourth of July the way fireworks exploded at Yankee Stadium, thanks to the short fuses of Lou Piniella and Carlton Fisk.

With the Yankees leading the Boston Red Sox 1–0 in the bottom of the sixth inning, the tense struggle erupted into a bench-clearing melee that sent one player to the hospital.

It happened right after Piniella tried to score from second base on a single. Boston right fielder Dwight Evans threw a perfect strike to Fisk to nail Piniella at the plate. Rather than slide, Piniella bowled into the burly catcher and tried to kick the ball away, but managed only to boot Fisk in the stomach. An upset Fisk responded by tagging Piniella again, this time on the head. In retaliation, Piniella grabbed Fisk by the chest protector, so Fisk socked him in the chin with the ball.

UPI/Bettmann Newsphotos

Naturally, the benches emptied and the players on both teams piled on top of Fisk and Piniella. For a moment, it looked like the umpires had kept the violence to a minimum, but then another fight broke out with two new combatants—Yankees third baseman Graig Nettles and Red Sox reliever Bill Lee.

Nettles put both arms around Lee and tried to drag him away from the Fisk-Piniella bout. Then New York outfielder Mickey Rivers jumped Lee from behind, put an arm around the pitcher's neck, and began punching him. Nettles and Lee fell to the ground. Nettles sprang to his feet and, facing a menacing group of Red Sox players, told them he was only trying to pry Lee off the pile.

Recalled Nettles, "Now, I'm one of the easiest-going guys you can find, but as I started to leave, Lee began yelling at me. I was going to ignore him, but he lost his head and started screaming at me. I couldn't take it any longer so I socked him in the eye, and he hit me."

Nettles and Lee were both thrown out of the game. But Lee paid a much stiffer price for his fighting. He tottered off the field, holding his left arm and wincing in pain. Taken to the hospital, Lee learned that ligaments in his shoulder were ripped and he was placed on the disabled list. Lee never regained his top form as a reliever.

Shaken and angered by the brawl, the Red Sox let their bats do the clobbering. Boston blasted three homers and a triple for eight runs in the last three innings to knock out the Yankees, 8–2.

Umpire Jocko Conlan *vs.*
Coach Leo Durocher

Los Angeles • April 16, 1961

Volatile Leo Durocher usually argued with umpires chin to chin, but on one wild Sunday afternoon, Leo the Lip tangled with arbiter Jocko Conlan *shin to shin*.

Not content to just jaw at each other in an argument at home plate, the two veteran bantams of the National League kept kicking each other where it really stings.

The outburst erupted during the fourth inning of a game between the visiting Pittsburgh Pirates and the Los Angeles Dodgers at the Coliseum. L.A. first baseman Norm Larker hit a pop-up that landed in fair territory between home and first but bounced foul. Conlan, claiming that no one had touched the ball in fair ground, called it a foul. Durocher, who had recently joined the Dodgers as a coach after a five-year absence from baseball, exploded in anger. He, along with the rest of his players, contended that Pirates catcher Hal Smith had touched the ball before it went foul.

After losing the argument, Durocher returned to the dugout where he tossed a towel in disgust. Jocko shouted, "You're out of the game!"

"You're ejecting me for throwing a towel in the dugout—our own dug-out?" Leo asked incredulously.

"You can't throw towels," Conlan snapped back.

"Oh, yeah? I can't do this, huh?" retorted Durocher, flinging a towel and a helmet onto the field. Then the irate coach charged the veteran umpire at home plate.

Standing toe to toe, the two engaged in a heated, curse-filled rhubarb. It escalated into an unforgettable bout when Leo kicked dirt all over the bottom of Conlan's trousers. Jocko, apparently unhappy at the thought of the cleaning bill, tried to kick some dirt back. But his shoe skidded off the ground and he booted Durocher right in the shin. So Leo retaliated with a nicely placed kick to Conlan's leg and the shin-kicking donnybrook was on. But when Jocko threw down his chest protector and mask, the other umpires separated the kicking combatants.

While observers called the match a draw, the unofficial nod had to go to Conlan. Like most home plate umpires, he wore shin guards and iron-plated toes in his shoes to protect him from foul balls. Recalled Durocher, who received a three-day suspension for his part in the shin-to-shin duel, "Every time Jocko kicked me, he raised a lump on my shins. Every time I kicked him, I bruised my toes. All at once it occurred to me that these were the lousiest odds I'd ever been up against."

First Bout: Hack Wilson vs. Ray Kolp
Second Bout: Hack Wilson vs. Pete Donohue

Chicago • July 4, 1929

Hack Wilson could usually hit the ball on the nose. But one memorable day, the pudgy Chicago Cubs slugger hit two Cincinnati Reds *pitchers* on the nose.

His big day as a pugilist began during the second game of a doubleheader at Wrigley Field. Throughout the opener and the nightcap, Wilson had been heckled unmercifully from the Reds' dugout by pitcher Ray Kolp.

Hack was fed up with the harassment and he waited for the right moment to get even. Leading off the bottom of the fifth inning, he lashed a single. As he reached first base, Wilson received an earful of abuse from Kolp, who wound up daring him to step into the dugout. Without even waiting to call time out, Hack sprinted into the dugout and clouted Kolp on the schnozz. Then Wilson tried to rip the uniforms off all the Reds who came near him.

His Chicago teammates charged across the field to back Hack up as fans spilled out onto the field. There was no doubt among fight observers that Kolp was counted out. However, Wilson was out, too. Because he neglected to call time, Hack was tagged out by third baseman Chuck Dressen during the middle of the melee.

Meanwhile, big, burly home plate umpire Cy Rigler fought his way through the fans who had clustered around the dugout. After restoring order, he ejected both Wilson and Kolp from the game. Hack was escorted to the Cub dugout by a policeman while Kolp was led away sporting a black eye.

For Wilson, who could swing his fists as fast as his bat, the brawl was only a matinee. He headlined an evening bout a few hours later—at the train station.

As luck would have it, both teams were scheduled to head east on the same train, the Gotham Limited. While the two clubs mingled at the boarding gate, Wilson was still hacked over the afternoon fight at the ball park. Marching up to a group of Cincy players, he snarled, "I'm coming into your car and make Kolp apologize to me."

Reds pitcher Pete Donohue stepped forward and, in a threatening voice, retorted, "You might not leave the car alive if you so much as stick your head inside."

"What's it to you?" snapped Wilson. "It's between Kolp and me. But if you want to get in on this, okay . . ." With that said, Hack hauled off and socked Donohue in the nose, sending him sprawling to the concrete floor. Donohue scrambled to his feet only to get decked again by Wilson. By then, players from both sides pulled the two apart.

To avert an all-night battle, railroad officials put the Reds in a car in the front of the train and sent the Cubs into a car toward the back.

Pat "The Karate Kid" Corrales
vs. Dave "The Ninja" Stewart

Oakland • July 1, 1986

This was not your typical basebrawl, unless you hail from the Orient. The combatants looked like losers in an audition for extras in a Bruce Lee movie.

Baseball spectators had never witnessed a martial arts bout on the field until Cleveland Indians manager Pat Corrales, a brown belt in karate, squared off against Oakland A's reliever Dave Stewart, a practitioner of Tae Kwon Do.

Fists and feet flew in the seventh inning of Cleveland's 9–0 rout over the A's in Oakland. Stewart had just served up a gopher ball to Tony Bernazard, one of five Indian round-trippers, when Julio Franco stepped into the batter's box. To no one's surprise, Stewart fired a high and tight fastball that nearly beaned Franco.

Plate umpire Derryl Cousins warned both benches that any more "pur-

pose" pitches would result in ejections. But that wasn't good enough for Corrales. He wanted Stewart thrown out of the game. But when the ump refused, the feisty manager attempted to eject Stewart himself.

After exchanging obscenities with each other, Corrales headed for the mound and Stewart met him halfway. Corrales (a.k.a. "The Karate Kid") attacked first. He delivered a weak kick to Stewart's ribs. The kick left Corrales off balance and an easy target for "The Ninja," who sent him sprawling to the turf with a crushing right cross to the jaw. The only thing typical about the fight was the obligatory emptying-of-the-dugouts followed by a ten-minute fracas that left three players injured, none seriously. Corrales, Stewart, and A's acting manager Jeff Newman were ejected. The league slapped Corrales and Stewart with four-day suspensions and $500 fines.

Nursing a bruised cheek after the game, Corrales recounted the battle. "I told Stewart I wasn't going to put up with that [beanballs]. He told me to come on out there, so I went. The man is twenty-eight and I'm forty-five, but I don't care. He tagged me pretty good. Maybe it wasn't too smart, but I had to do it."

In the A's locker room, Stewart denied he deliberately threw at Franco's head, and blamed Corrales for instigating the fight. "He was screaming obscenities at me and I got tired of it, so I told him, 'Come on out here,'" said Stewart. "He tried to kick me in the ribs, but there wasn't much impact.

"What kind of guy does that? A sissy. I've heard a lot of good things about Corrales, but he showed me nothing by using his foot. What he showed me is that he's a coward. Maybe it's old age. Maybe he thought that was the only way he could defend himself against me. He's a woman."

BULLPEN BOZOS

The job of relief pitchers is to kill rallies. But usually all they kill is time. Stuck in a bullpen far removed from the on-field action and the rest of the team, these oddballs give the baseball world reason to question their sanity. They fight boredom by concentrating less on the game and more on pulling wild pranks, eating smuggled hot dogs, and making dates with pretty bleacherites. For "The Most Outrageous Performances by Relief Pitchers," The Baseball Hall of SHAME inducts the following:

The Cuckoo's Nest

Texas, A.L. • 1979–80

During 1979 and 1980, the Texas Rangers' bullpen was known more for comic relief than strong relief. That's why fans named it the Cuckoo's Nest.

The two aces of the bullpen—Jim Kern and Sparky Lyle—were jokers who enjoyed such pranks as torching players' shoes, sabotaging jockstraps, putting goldfish in the water cooler of the opposing bullpen, and stripping for fans.

They even set up a blind date for a teammate during a game. "We were always sneaking binoculars into the bullpen to watch the pretty girls in the stands," Kern recalled. "It was illegal to have binoculars because the league thought you would use them to steal the other team's signs. We really didn't give a damn about that.

"One hot summer day, Sparky and I were using them to check out the girls in their short shorts and tanktops when I spotted this good-looking chick staring right back at me through her binoculars. We got some paper and a felt marker and wrote, 'Would you like a date with [relief pitcher] Dave Rajsich?' She tore a popcorn box and wrote on it, 'Yes!'

"We told Razor [Dave's nickname], but he didn't believe us. So we got her to stand up and he just about fainted. Here were thousands of fans thinking we're in the bullpen concentrating on the game, waiting to come in for some last-minute heroics. Yet all this time we were setting up a blind date for Razor via binoculars. He kept that date, too."

Sometimes the players tried scientific experiments. Before one game, they ate nachos and soda and let the mess drip down their chins. They wanted to see if the fans in the front row would throw up.

The Ranger relievers tried to make rookies feel welcome. When one young pitcher was called into the game, he eagerly grabbed for his glove as he started for the mound. He almost dislocated his shoulder. His glove had been nailed to the bullpen bench.

On the field, members of the Cuckoo's Nest gave it their all. Especially Sparky Lyle. During batting practice before a game in July 1980, Lyle tossed a baseball into the bleachers to a begging group of Little Leaguers. When they shouted, "More! More!" Sparky obliged them with a few more balls. Then a girl yelled, "Hey, Sparky, can I have your hat?" Lyle nodded and fired his cap into the stands. Next, someone yelled, "How about throwing me your glove, Sparky." So Lyle flipped his glove to the fan. By now Sparky was on a roll. He unbuttoned his shirt and tossed that to the crowd. Then he removed his sweatshirt, trousers, shoes, and socks and threw them into the stands. Not until he was down to his shorts did Lyle quit stripping. He strutted off the field in his underwear to a standing ovation from the bleacher fans.

Lyle and Kern acted as if they were roommates from the same padded cell. "Playing baseball is much easier if everyone thinks you're an off-the-wall babbling idiot," said Kern, who was nicknamed "the Amazing Emu" because of his resemblance to the tall, skinny Australian bird. Whenever the 6-foot, 5-inch pitcher walked into the clubhouse, he was greeted with low-pitched cries of "Emu, Emu." Jim responded by making bloodcurdling vulture calls.

"Everyone considers relief pitchers nuts," he said. "You have to be or else you couldn't survive. You have to take a slightly cockeyed look at life."

His daffy philosophy was born in the minors during a memorable game. "We were winning 9–0 in the bottom of the eighth inning," Jim recalled. "I was with the other relievers down in the bullpen trading baseballs with the bleacher fans for hot dogs, sodas, and peanuts. We didn't think there was any chance of us getting used in the game so we stuffed ourselves like pigs and managed to give away all the balls. Suddenly, the other team scored five runs in the ninth and I got the word to warm up. I couldn't have pitched if my life depended on it because I was so bloated. Besides, we didn't have any balls left. Then I got an idea. It was real dark down there and we didn't have a bullpen coach. So I told the catcher to just pretend to catch while I pretended to throw. The bleacher fans thought we were nuts warming up without a ball. It was about a week before management found out and fined us $250."

When Kern joined the Cleveland Indians, he learned the wacky facts of bullpen life from such flakes as Fritz Peterson, John Lowenstein, and Gaylord Perry. In the Municipal Stadium bullpen, the relievers killed moths and put them in spiderwebs. "Then we'd spend an inning watching the spider catch the moth and eat it," Jim recalled. "We each had a spider and it was a contest to see who could grow the biggest one. We wanted to get one big enough so it could answer the phone and warm up five guys at once."

When Kern was traded to the Texas Rangers in 1979, he made a fiery first impression. He set rookie Danny Darwin's shoes ablaze. "I dipped cotton balls in alcohol, rubbed it all over his shoes, and when I put a match to 'em, they went up like a forest fire," Jim recalled with pride.

Kern mastered the subtle art of surreptitiously coating teammates' jock-straps with a liniment that left a burning sensation in the most tender part of their anatomy. "You could always tell who the victim was because he walked funny," Jim said.

No one was safe from Kern, even away from the stadium. During a road trip in Minneapolis, Jim stole some room keys from the team hotel, barged into teammates' rooms, and sprayed them with a fire extinguisher.

On a Ranger flight, Jim noticed that one of the sportswriters covering the team was reading the last chapter of John Dean's book, *Blind Ambition*. Perhaps hungry for food for thought, Kern grabbed the book away from the writer, ripped out the final pages, and ate them. "There," Jim said. "Now figure out how it ends."

Ron Perranoski

Pitcher • Los Angeles, N.L. • 1964

Ron Perranoski found a shameful way to cool off the ardor of young fans who dared ask the Los Angeles Dodgers relief ace for an autograph when he was in the bullpen.

During a game at Dodger Stadium, eleven-year-old Scott Kaufer was dying to get an autograph from Perranoski, one of his favorite stars. So Scott marched down toward the left-field bullpen and shoved his scorecard and pen through the chainlink fence that separated the relievers from the fans.

Perranoski was sitting on a chair with his arms folded, staring at the action on the field.

"Can I have your autograph, Mr. Perranoski?" Scott asked innocently and politely.

The reliever turned around and viewed the bright-eyed boy with annoyance. "Can't sign during the game," he said. "League rules." Then in one motion, Perranoski reached in his warm-up jacket, pulled out a water pistol, and squirted Scott in the face. The pitcher quickly stuck the gun back in his pocket, folded his arms, and resumed watching the game.

Kaufer, who is now a television industry executive, recalled, "Like any kid, I was just thankful for the contact with a major leaguer—no matter what. I told Perranoski, 'Thank you,' and then I wiped my face and walked away."

Will McEnaney

Pitcher • Pittsburgh, N.L. • September 17, 1978

Will McEnaney literally double-crossed his manager.

During a game against the visiting Montreal Expos, Pittsburgh Pirates manager Chuck Tanner thought he could see his left-handed reliever sitting in the bullpen. Actually, Will was relaxing in the clubhouse watching a football game the entire time. Then who was wearing his uniform out in the bullpen? Will's twin brother, Mike.

"We planned it all out," the prankish Will recalled. "We're identical twins and we used to do things like this all the time when we were growing up. We switched classes, girlfriends, and Little League uniforms but never got caught."

Will concocted the scheme because his mind was on football even though the Pirates were in the thick of a pennant race. He was determined to watch the Pittsburgh Steelers play the Cincinnati Bengals on TV. But the gridiron battle was slated to start at the same time as the baseball game.

In a stroke of luck, Mike paid him a visit at the Three Rivers Stadium clubhouse before the game began. Mike mentioned that he'd never been in the dugout or bullpen during a major league game.

"You will today," said Will, eagerly handing over his Pirates uniform. "This is the perfect opportunity. Now I can watch the football game."

In a leery voice, Mike said, "I don't think we can get away with this."

"Sure we can. No one is going to find out. Go out to the bullpen for about five or six innings and then come back and I'll take your place."

"What if Tanner calls on me—or rather you—to pitch?"

"If they ask you to warm up, just tell them you have to go to the bathroom first. Then hustle back here to the clubhouse and we'll change. But don't worry. Tanner and I aren't getting along at all, so I really don't expect to be called."

Satisfied but still somewhat nervous, Mike donned his brother's uniform and pretended to be a Pirate. No one caught on to the switch. However, Pittsburgh captain Willie Stargell kept staring at Mike in the dugout during the playing of the national anthem, trying to figure out what was different about him. But then Stargell turned his attention to the game as Mike headed for the bullpen.

The brothers McEnaney got away with their scam. Will watched most of the football game and Mike got to sit in the bullpen in uniform during a major league game.

Recalled Mike, "Kids kept leaning over the railing of the bullpen, yelling, 'Hey, Will, give us your autograph.' So I did. I wonder how much a Will McEnaney autograph signed by Mike McEnaney is worth?"

Dave LaRoche

Pitcher • California-Minnesota-Cleveland-New York, A.L.; Chicago, N.L. • 1970–83

As a journeyman reliever, Dave LaRoche was supposed to put out fires, not start them.

But that's exactly what he did shortly after he was traded to the Cleveland Indians in 1975. Shivering out in the Municipal Stadium bullpen in a chilling April wind, LaRoche turned to his fellow relievers and said, "We need a fire to stay warm." They all agreed, so he started a small blaze with some newspapers and old scorecards. Dave and the other players warmed their hands. But then the flames set the bullpen bench on fire, sending up a trail of smoke that could be seen by everyone in the park.

When the fire was finally extinguished, bullpen coach Jeff Torborg told LaRoche, "You guys better enjoy this."

"Why?" Dave asked.

"Because," answered Torborg, "it may cost more than you think to buy this town a new bullpen."

In 1981, when he was with the Yankees, LaRoche took his role as a fireman a little more seriously. During the middle of a game, Dave grabbed a hose and watered down everybody in the bullpen. "We were kind of expecting it," said pitcher Rudy May. "He'd been looking funny at that hose all year. I mean, what's a fireman without a hose?"

With tongue firmly in cheek, May added, "Dave has always tended to be what you'd call a source of problems." May should know. He was LaRoche's teammate in the early 1970s when both were with the California Angels. During one game, while the two were warming up, May was summoned from the bullpen to pitch. But LaRoche decided that he, too, was ready, so he sauntered to the mound with May. Fans, players, and umpires couldn't believe their eyes. *Two* hurlers were on the mound ready to pitch. Of course, the rules prohibit a pitching duet, so LaRoche was sent back to the bullpen.

That wasn't the only time Dave proved he was a class-A flake. During another game, he wanted to convince the bullpen coach that he was loose. So LaRoche threw the ball over 300 feet and hit the twenty-three-story-tall scoreboard in Anaheim Stadium. Right after his throw struck it, the million-dollar electronic scoreboard started flashing hieroglyphics.

Dave had a thing for scoreboards. In 1975 when he was with Cleveland,

LaRoche failed to show up for a workout. Recalled Jeff Torborg, who was the bullpen coach at the time, "We were worried about Dave until we saw him, in uniform, waving to us from the top of the scoreboard. He told us it was a clear day and he just wanted to see the Cleveland skyline."

The Bullpen Wars:
Kansas City Royals vs. Baltimore Orioles
1969

Never in the history of baseball have two bullpen crews battled in such an utterly wacky season-long war.

Both sides engaged in hit-and-run guerrilla tactics, wielding such devastating weapons as cherry bombs, dirt balls, and stones. One side even resorted to chemical warfare.

The battle cry was sounded after relief pitcher and prankster Moe Drabowsky went from the Baltimore Orioles to the fledgling Kansas City Royals in the expansion draft of 1969. Throughout the year, Drabowsky rallied the Royals' bullpen troops while O's pitchers Pete Richert and Eddie Watt directed the Baltimore corps' retaliatory measures.

On May 10, 1969, Moe launched the first commando raid on the O's bullpen during a night game at Baltimore's Memorial Stadium. The Royals' bullpen squad synchronized their watches for an assault at 2130 hours (9:30 P.M. for nonmilitary types) or about the fourth inning. The attack force consisted of pitchers Wally Bunker, Bill Butler, Mike Hedlund, Jim Rooker, and catcher Buck Martinez.

"I had our guys ready to go," Drabowsky recalled. "We blackened our faces with burnt cork and wore dark jackets. Our pockets were loaded with simulated hand grenades—rocks and dirt balls. We snuck around the corner of our bullpen in right center, darted through the trees in center field behind the scoreboard, crept and crawled through the grass, and maneuvered into a strategic position behind the Baltimore bullpen in left center.

"When we were all in place, I gave the signal and we opened fire. Bombs away! We kept our arms in shape by grenading the bullpen. The rocks hit the roof and back wall of their shelter and made a hell of a racket. You should have seen them jump. They were cussing and screaming in rage over this sneak attack."

Two days later, the O's launched a counteroffensive. In the third inning of an afternoon game, Richert and Watt slipped behind the scoreboard and outfield hedge and lofted an earsplitting firecracker that sent the startled Royals leaping out of their bullpen shed.

"I knew it had to be Watt and Richert," said Drabowsky. "They were the only ones crazy enough to do it. It had to be Watt who threw the firecracker, because his control had been off. The thing landed twenty feet away from the shed.

"I didn't see them coming because I didn't think they'd be dumb enough to attack us in broad daylight where God and everybody could see them. They didn't have enough sense to wait for a night game."

The O's counterattack backfired. Since Richert and Watt were not as experienced as Moe in waging war, their afternoon raid was clearly seen from the press box by reporters—and Harry Dalton, the Orioles personnel director. When he saw two O's caps bobbing behind the hedge, Dalton telephoned bullpen coach Charlie Lau and told him in no uncertain terms, "No more foolishness."

The Baltimore bullpen expected Drabowsky to retaliate. He didn't disappoint them. When the Orioles walked into the visitors' clubhouse in Kansas City five days later, they were repulsed by a horrible odor. The sneaky Moe had placed a foul-smelling chemical in the ventilation system.

Early the next morning, hours before game time, Richert and Watt sought revenge. They painted the Royals' bullpen pitching rubbers and plates black and orange, the Orioles' colors.

Drabowsky felt duty-bound to strike back again. This time he was accused of putting sneezing powder in the air-conditioning system of the Baltimore clubhouse because the Orioles were sneezing as they suited up for the game.

This provocation did not go unanswered. When the Royals went out to their bullpen the next day, they discovered that the roof of their shelter was no longer dark green. It was now bright orange—*wet,* bright orange—with the words *Go Birds* printed on the roof.

Moe fired the final salvo of the year. On the first day of the 1969 World Series in Baltimore, a plane circled over Memorial Stadium and pulled a banner with a message directed to the O's bullpen crew: "Good luck, Birds. Beware of Moe."

THE BLIGHTS OF SPRING

Spring training is a time when players are supposed to work out all the winter kinks and fine-tune their baseball skills. But six weeks in the warmth of Florida or the Southwest doesn't seem to help some guys. For them, getting into shape is a matter of mind over matter. They don't mind goofing off, so it doesn't matter how badly they perform in the preseason. For "The Most Foolish Behavior in Spring Training," The Baseball Hall of SHAME inducts the following:

Ping Bodie

Outfielder • New York, A.L. • April 3, 1919

Eat to win is nothing new. Ping Bodie was doing it decades ago. Only it had nothing to do with nutrition.

Bodie, the 5-foot, 8-inch, 195-pound roommate of Babe Ruth, handled a knife and fork with more skill than a bat and ball. The roly-poly outfielder could cover more ground at the training table than Joe DiMaggio did in center field.

Ping's most ludicrous gastronomical feat occurred in 1919 at the Yankees spring training camp in Jacksonville, Florida, when he challenged an ostrich named Percy to the heavyweight spaghetti-eating championship of the world.

In front of a packed house at the South Side Pavilion, a local hall, Yankees co-owner Til Huston, who footed the fodder bills for Bodie, introduced his trencherman to the cheering crowd. Ping bowed gracefully after stepping into a boxing ring where the eating event was about to take place. Truck Hannah, the team's 190-pound catcher and gorger, acted as Bodie's second.

Then the ostrich, sponsored by the Jacksonville Chamber of Commerce, was led in by Brooklyn Dodgers manager Wilbert Robinson, himself a legendary greedygut who consented to second for Percy.

Ping scowled defiantly at his feathered opponent while the ostrich sharpened his beak on the canvas and playfully poked Robinson in his jelly belly.

The match, which was not advertised for fear of arousing the wrath of animal lovers, would determine whether Percy or Bodie could eat the most plates of spaghetti. The following is a round-by-round, firsthand account:

Round 1

Both platters were cleaned seconds after the bell rang. Ping was a trifle disconcerted by a sprig of spaghetti that eluded his fork, but he grasped it in his hands and flung the fork out of the ring.

Round 2

Once again, Bodie cleaned his plate in less than a minute while Percy seemed to tarry a bit. Experts began to figure that Percy—billed as the world's greatest eater—had met his match at last. Members of the Chamber of Commerce, who had wagered heavily on the contest, began to look for a chance to hedge their bets.

Round 3

The ostrich came back strong in this round and swallowed his second's watch and chain with the third platter. But the smile of confidence remained upon Bodie's face. Members of the Yankee team shouted, "Stay with him, Ping!" Bodie sneered at the ostrich as he went to his corner.

Round 4

The ostrich showed signs of punishment in this round. Percy's sides had begun to swell visibly, while Ping showed not an ounce of trouble.

Round 5

The ostrich came out a bit weary. Bodie's golden smile widened, and he refused the napkin offered by his solicitous second.

Round 6

Percy was tiring visibly. Many female spectators at ringside started for the door because they couldn't stomach seeing the finish.

Round 7

Even strong men began to edge back from the ring. They began to fear that in a few more rounds Percy would explode.

Round 8

It was plain even to the layman that Ping was merrily munching on his food while Percy the ostrich was dying on his feet.

Round 9

At the start of the round, even hardened eaters were shouting to Wilbert Robinson to throw in the napkin. "Do you want your bird killed?" they demanded. Robinson retorted brutally, "He won't quit while he's on his feet."

Round 10

The ostrich staggered out of his corner with his beak sagging. It was plain that he had little left. Bodie just grinned.

Round 11

Percy barely waddled out from his corner. The ostrich's eyes were blood-shot and his sides were heaving as he toed his platter. He was a badly beaten bird. Ping was almost finished with his platter when Percy dropped to his knees. The timekeeper began to count. Bodie ferociously downed the last morsel and stepped back to survey his fallen opponent. As the time-keeper muttered the final "ten," the ostrich keeled over to rise no more.

Ping was then declared the undisputed spaghetti-eating champion of the world.

Mike Schmidt

Third Baseman • Philadelphia, N.L. • March 25, 1977

For a superstar, Mike Schmidt should have been ashamed of himself. He failed to buckle down in spring training camp.

Schmidt revealed his true self during morning exercises at the Philadelphia Phillies' training camp in Clearwater, Florida. The team's special conditioning coach, Gus Hoefling, a stickler for timeliness, had ordered the players to begin their stretching exercises.

But Schmidt was still dallying in the clubhouse while putting on his uniform. When he heard Hoefling bark out the cadence to the first exercise, Mike was literally caught with his pants down. So Schmidt dropped what he was doing and waddled out onto the field with his unbuckled, unzipped pants down around his knees. All alone in the back row, he joined in a neck-stretching exercise and didn't "waist" any time by fastening his pants.

Some fans thought that displaying his backside was a cheeky thing to do. But Schmidt felt that spring training is the best time for a player to show his

stuff. The long and the shorts of this controversy came down to this: with all the razzing Schmidt received, it was a cinch he would've rather shown off his MVP trophies than his BVD skivvies.

Ron "Rocky" Swoboda

Outfielder • New York, N.L. • 1965–70

For Rocky Swoboda, spring training could be just as cruel as a winter blizzard. He was snowed under by one hilariously shameful moment after another.

In a game during his first spring training with the Mets, Swoboda hit a foul pop-up behind the plate. Rather than move out of the way, Rocky stayed put and, in utter fascination, watched the catcher circle under the ball. Too bad Swoboda wasn't watching the ball—because it came down and hit him right on his head.

There was no doubt among baseball observers that Rocky was born to be a Met.

During spring training in 1967, Swoboda turned into a caged tiger. In a game against the New York Yankees at Fort Lauderdale, Met manager Wes Westrum sent one of his coaches down to the batting cage to summon Rocky to pinch-hit. Swoboda was taking some extra cuts in the cage. When he received word that Westrum wanted him, Rocky eagerly reached for the batting-cage door. But in his haste, he accidentally pulled the chain that locked the cage and, to his chagrin, found himself trapped. After yanking and yanking, Swoboda finally had to break the lock with his bat. But by the time Rocky freed himself, Westrum had tired of waiting and sent up another batter to pinch-hit.

The following year, Swoboda did a disappearing act in the middle of a spring training game against the Baltimore Orioles in Miami. In the third inning, Rocky was due up at the plate but was nowhere to be found. Manager Gil Hodges looked up and down the bench in vain. No Swoboda. He looked in the runway leading to the dressing room. No Swoboda. So Hodges sent Cleon Jones up to pinch-hit for Rocky. Where was Swoboda? He was in the bathroom taking a crap.

Lonny "Error-a-Day" Frey

Second Baseman • Cincinnati, N.L. • April 12, 1942

Lonny "Error-a-Day" Frey was a bit too patriotic during the last spring training game of 1942.

Playing at home against the Detroit Tigers, the Cincinnati Reds took to the field for the start of the game. The players paused for the traditional playing of "The Star Spangled Banner," but the public address system malfunctioned, so play began without honoring the flag.

Tigers' leadoff man Jimmy Bloodworth then swatted an easy grounder toward Frey. As Frey bent over to field the ball, the public address system operator finished repairing the equipment. Suddenly, the loudspeakers blared, "Oh, say, can you see . . ."

At the sound of the anthem, Frey dutifully stopped, doffed his cap, and stood at attention. The ground ball proceeded to bounce right past him for a single.

"When the anthem started playing, I stopped running down toward first," recalled Bloodworth. "But then I figured I'd better run it out. If Lonny hadn't been so patriotic, I wouldn't have had a hit."

You're Out, Ump!

Umpires are necessary evils like batting slumps, bad-hop singles, and cold hot dogs. Without them, what would fans have to complain about? Grudgingly, we must admit that umpires are pretty honest fellows. It's just that the men in blue occasionally screw up and strike out like the rest of us. For "The Most Deplorable Actions by Umpires," The Baseball Hall of SHAME inducts the following:

Ted Hendry

Umpire, A.L. • April 13, 1980

Of all the performances of the umpiring crew during an early-season game, Ted Hendry shamefully brought up the rear.

The bare fact is that he officiated a major league game with his pants and underwear ripped wide open.

Hendry had put on a new uniform to work home plate in the Seattle Mariners–Toronto Blue Jays game in the Kingdome. However, when he took his position in the first inning and bent over, the seam in the seat of his pants split. Not only that, but his white shorts were torn in the fanny, too. And he didn't know it.

Fans in the box seats behind home plate knew it. They were in stitches, even though it was Hendry who needed a tailor. At the end of the inning, he was politely informed that he was the butt of all the cackles.

Red-faced, the umpire scurried off to the dressing room for repairs. He returned decorated with a safety pin in the offending area. Although his dignity was hurt, that was nothing compared to how his rear felt. That's because when Hendry bent over, the pin pricked him. The ump bravely lasted until the third inning when he was again forced to mend his ways in the dressing room.

Hendry returned to call balls and strikes but, to his dismay, the pin would not hold, making it a truly revealing situation. By the bottom of the sixth inning, Hendry could no longer officiate by the seat of his pants and ran off the field for the third time.

Hendry obviously wasn't capable of fixing the situation on his own. So Seattle general manager Lou Gorman dug up a pair of blue cutoffs, which Hendry put on under his torn pants. At least this way only blue showed through the split. Hendry managed to finish the game without further incident—and then tried to put the mortifying matter behind him.

Charlie Williams

Umpire, N.L. • June 5–6, 1986

Umpire Charlie Williams deserves the thumb for ruining the all-time nice-guy record of Steve Garvey.

Williams had the audacity to label the San Diego Padres first baseman a troublemaker. The ump actually had the nerve to eject baseball's Mr. Clean from a game for the first time in his career—and that counts Little League through 2,201 major league contests.

Garvey's first-ever ouster came on June 5 during a home game against the Atlanta Braves. Garvey was in the on-deck circle in the third inning when teammate Bip Roberts dove across home plate, apparently scoring. How-

ever, Williams made no call, then signaled Roberts out when Braves catcher Ozzie Virgil belatedly applied the tag.

Garvey protested and used his bat to circle a mark in the dirt, showing Williams where Roberts' hand had brushed across the plate. Then horror of horrors, Garvey said not one but two four-letter words! He shouted at the ump, "Bear down!" Pretty strong language for Garvey, but hardly ear-numbing for a nun let alone a major league umpire. However, it was enough for Williams. Besides, said the ump, "He showed me up at home plate. He had no business drawing pictures down there on the ground."

Garvey was understandably upset over the boot. "It's unbelievable," he said after the game. "I didn't say anything bad. I just showed Williams where Bip's hand hit the plate. I've been playing ball for thirty years and have never been thrown out of a game. I've never cussed an umpire."

San Diego manager Steve Boros, who also rushed to the plate to argue the call, peppered Williams with a slew of choice words (none of which were the heinous "bear down"). During the squabble, the ump told the manager, "I'll look at any replay you've got. I didn't miss that call."

Boros decided to take up the arbiter's offer after viewing TV replays which showed that Roberts had indeed dusted the bottom of the plate with his hand. So the next night, Boros walked to home plate for the presentation of the lineup cards, then turned to Williams and tried to hand him a video tape of the play in question. The incensed ump promptly booted Boros out of the game before it even began.

"I'm not proud of what I did," said Boros, who was later fined $200 by the league. "But it was something I had to do. Any ump can miss a call, but he had no right to throw Garvey out so fast. That's what I was upset about. Every fifteen years, I just go wild. It must have something to do with the alignment of the planets."

The following night, the San Diego fans decided to let Williams know what they thought about his quick thumb. An airplane flying over the stadium trailed a banner that read, "Impeach Umpire Williams." Then another plane dropped a giant pair of inflatable eyeglasses.

Emmett Ashford

Umpire, A.L. • August 4, 1968

Emmett Ashford made every call a Broadway production. He pirouetted, jumped, or pivoted before giving his decision in a booming voice.

But there was one time when the eccentric, roly-poly arbiter should have clammed up and not moved.

The Baltimore Orioles were beating the New York Yankees 5–3 in the bottom of the eighth inning when Joe Pepitone of the Yanks reached first base on an error. O's first sacker Boog Powell decided to try the old hidden-ball trick on the unsuspecting runner. Boog, who made it quite obvious that he had the ball in his glove, walked over to the pitching mound without calling time out. It was a ploy to lure Pepitone off the unprotected base. Powell then pretended to hand the ball to his pitcher, Eddie Watt.

With the ball hidden in his glove, Boog glanced over to Pepitone and was delighted to see that Joe had fallen for the fake and strayed off first. He was all set up. But then Ashford unthinkingly got in on the act. Umpiring at second base, he suddenly threw up his hands and yelled, "Time!"

Neither Watt nor Powell could believe his ears. "Emmett, why are you calling time?" Watt demanded.

"Because," answered Ashford, oblivious to the skulduggery, "Boog's got the ball and he forgot to call time. I'm just trying to be helpful."

Getting more steamed by the second, Watt glared at the smiling ump and shouted, "Thanks, Emmett. You just spoiled our plot for a surefire hidden-ball trick."

Then Powell chimed in. "Hell, Emmett. Didn't you know what we were doing? You really blew that one for us."

A relieved Joe Pepitone nodded in agreement—from his safe position back on first base.

Bill "Lord" Byron

Umpire, N.L. • 1913–19

No arbiter could taunt a protesting player better than Bill Byron, "The Singing Umpire."

Whenever a batter squawked at him on a called third strike, Byron would chant this favorite ditty:

> "Let me tell you something, son
> Before you get much older.
> You cannot hit the ball, my friend
> With the bat upon your shoulder."

The louder the harangue, the softer was Byron's smart-alecky song, unless the protester pushed him too far. Then Bill changed his tune—in more ways than one. He had a quick thumb and even quicker fists.

Hall of Fame second baseman Johnny Evers was silenced by one of Byron's tuneful putdowns. Sliding into second on an attempted steal, the Boston Brave was called out by Byron. "I'm safe!" yelled Evers, who then held his nose to indicate what he thought of the call.

Rather than argue, Byron just chanted, "It's a difference of opinion, difference of opinion; that's all I have to say."

But Evers had more to say, and he unleashed a string of invectives. So Byron, singing the melody of "In the Shade of the Old Apple Tree," responded with:

> "Go sit down with the other men.
> If you don't it will cost you ten.
> If you don't go away,
> It will cost you your pay
> While mine will go on, don't you see?"

Evers went to the bench and kept quiet for the rest of the game.

In prose or in verse, Byron was equal to every challenge that unfolded on the diamond. If the rules were on his side, he imperiously cited them. If not, he actually changed them to meet his needs. Take, for example, the time he made up a rule during a game in Baltimore. The Orioles had the bases loaded with two outs when the batter hit a foul pop-up near first base. O's coach Jack Dunn left the coaching box and kept yelling, "I've got it! I've got it!" The first baseman, tricked into thinking that a teammate was about to make the catch, stopped chasing the ball and it fell harmlessly to the ground.

To Dunn's surprise, Byron called the batter out. "For what?" Dunn screamed. "Interference," the umpire thundered. "What do you mean, interference?" demanded Dunn. "I mean *vocal* interference," ruled Byron.

Byron had little patience with argumentative players or managers. But sometimes he bullied them too much with his sharp tongue, quick temper, and rabbit punches. There was the game in Chicago in 1915 when he triggered a fight with Boston Braves third baseman Red Smith. Because Byron instigated the fracas, National League President John Tener ordered Byron to publicly apologize to the fans before the start of the next game. Byron meekly complied.

Byron's slurs brought him more trouble—and a bloody lip—two years later. He made the mistake of offending hot-tempered New York Giants manager John McGraw. At the end of a game in Cincinnati on June 8, 1917, Byron was confronted in front of the Giants clubhouse by a seething-mad McGraw, whom Byron had ejected two days in a row. After an exchange of words, Byron said, "You talk big. I guess you didn't used to be so tough. They say you were run out of Baltimore."

McGraw, fiercely proud of his achievement as a star third baseman for the Orioles, wouldn't stand for anybody telling such a black lie—even an umpire like Bill Byron. McGraw threw a short right punch that split Byron's upper lip. After players from both teams plunged into the fray, cops wrestled through the melee, pulled McGraw and Byron out, and led them to their dressing rooms.

Byron frequently incited howls and jeers from fans and was once the target of one of the strangest barrages ever thrown at an umpire. In 1915 in St. Louis, he banished a Cardinal player during a game against the Chicago

Cubs. The angered fans didn't throw pop bottles or garbage at Byron. They threw cucumbers! Apparently, that's what they thought Byron had for brains.

Bill Klem

Umpire, N.L. • April 25, 1913

Home plate umpire Bill Klem nullified the winning run of a game because it was scored behind his back—while he was announcing a pinch hitter to the crowd.

The stubborn arbiter literally stole a game that the New York Giants had won.

The play unfolded at the most critical moment of a scoreless tie with the visiting Philadelphia Phillies. New York had loaded the bases with one out in the bottom of the 10th inning when Moose McCormick was sent up to the plate to pinch-hit. As was the custom of the day, Klem turned his back to the field to announce that McCormick was batting for Giants pitcher Al Demaree.

While Klem was making the announcement, Phillies pitcher Grover Alexander fired a fastball that Moose swatted into left field for a single, driving in Fred Merkle from third base with the game-winning run. Cheering fans leaped onto the Polo Grounds field while the Giants happily trotted toward the clubhouse.

But Klem started shouting, "No! Positively no!" He said that Alexander and McCormick should have waited until he had told the 10,000 spectators that Moose was pinch-hitting. Since Klem had not finished his introduction when McCormick had swung, the ump ruled that the ball had not been in play. Klem ordered the Phillies back onto the field and McCormick to the batter's box.

However, Moose had already stripped off his uniform and was ready for the showers. So Klem hired a messenger boy to go into the clubhouse and tell McCormick that he must bat all over again. Moose was dumbfounded, but reluctantly put on his uniform and returned to the field. The base runners went back to their respective bases and McCormick stepped up to the plate again. But history did not repeat itself. Moose hit a grounder to first baseman Fred Luderus who threw home for the force-out on Merkle. Catcher Red Dooin then fired back to first for a nifty double play to end the inning. The game was called after the next inning because of darkness. The score was still 0–0.

Wrote *The New York Times* the next day: "If you were at the game and you are a resident of New York, way down in your heart you would have thought that the Giants had won fair and square. Sure, everybody thinks so. But don't overlook Mr. Klem . . . He holds the same position in baseball that the Czar of Russia holds in his bailiwick. The fact is, you can't beat him."

Eric Gregg

Umpire, N.L. • September 20, 1979

Eric Gregg was the only umpire who ever let a ball girl call a play for him. Worse than that, the call was wrong.

Gregg was working third base during a night game between the visiting Pittsburgh Pirates and the Philadelphia Phillies. In the bottom of the sixth inning with a 1–1 score, the Phillies had runners at first and second with one out and rookie Keith Moreland at the plate.

Moreland hit a screaming, rising liner down the left-field line and Gregg looked up into the lights of Veterans Stadium trying to follow the flight of the ball. But the lights were so bright that the ump was momentarily blinded.

"The next thing I knew the ball was gone and I saw absolutely nothing," Gregg recalled. "Finally I saw Mary Sue Styles, a beautiful Phillies ball girl, jumping up and down and yelling, 'Home run! Home run!' I said to myself, 'Eric, if it's good enough for her, it's good enough for me.' Besides, she's a fox. So I signaled home run."

The Pirates jumped all over Gregg, insisting that even the eyes of a potato could see that the ball landed foul. "The Pirates circled me so fast I felt like Ward Bond in 'Wagon Train,'" Gregg said. "I turned to look for my source for help. But Mary Sue had vanished."

Gregg then huddled with the rest of the umpiring crew and confessed that he hadn't seen the ball. His colleagues agreed that the ball was foul, negating what would have been Moreland's first major league homer. Home plate umpire Doug Harvey then asked Gregg, "Do you want to change the call or do you want me to?"

Gregg looked up in the stands at the angry spectators who were screaming vile epithets at him for even questioning Moreland's swat. Without hesitation, Gregg told Harvey, "You change it."

Although Gregg lives in Philadelphia, the fans there treat him no differently than they do the other umps. "Once I called [Phillies shortstop] Larry Bowa out on a close play and 40,000 people booed me," Gregg said. "I looked up in the stands to my wife for comfort. She threw her hands at me in disgust."

ROUND TRIP-UPS

The home run slugger's only regret in life is that he can't sit in the stands and watch himself belt a four-bagger. Perhaps that's a good thing because not all homers deserve to be applauded. Although they look good in the box score, some round-trippers deserve to be booed. For The Most Shameful Home Runs of All Time,"The Baseball Hall of SHAME inducts the following:

Reggie Jackson's Homer

September 23, 1981

Reggie Jackson was not content to belt a home run off pitcher John Denny. He tried to belt Denny, too.

As a result, Jackson's four-bagger ended in a two-round brawl—and in shame.

The New York Yankees were playing at home against the Cleveland Indians when Denny first infuriated Jackson in the second inning. The hurler threw a high fastball under Reggie's chin, then struck him out two pitches later. Jackson, who had been decked several times by brushback pitches the previous week, charged the mound. Players from both sides spilled out of the dugouts and onto the field, but no punches were thrown. Yankee teammates Bobby Brown and Oscar Gamble grabbed the enraged Reggie and dragged him back to the dugout.

Jackson was determined to get even with Denny during his next at-bat in the fourth inning. Sure enough, Reggie ripped a 2–2 pitch into the right-field bleachers for a two-run homer that gave the Yanks a 6–1 lead.

With a cocky grin on his face. Jackson paused in the batter's box long enough to pump his fist defiantly at Denny, then tipped his cap to the cheering crowd as he circled the bases. Meanwhile, in the middle of the diamond, a seething-mad Denny stared at Reggie during his home run trot and the two adversaries swapped taunts.

After stepping on home plate, Jackson suddenly turned and ran at Denny, grabbing the pitcher around the head and wrestling him to the ground. Once again, players and coaches left the dugouts and bullpens, but this time they engaged in a punching, clawing brawl. For the second time that night, Jackson was hauled away from the fracas by Brown and Gamble. Carried like a surfboard, Reggie clapped and cheered for his triumph on the way to the dugout. Gamble, who had been benched because of a hitting slump, said later, "I guess I've found a new job with the Yankees. But if I'm going to keep taking Reggie out, he's got to lose weight."

Jackson reappeared from the dugout seconds later with his uniform shirt off. He was ready for another round. Taking up the challenge, Indians catcher Ron Hassey threw off his chest protector and headed toward him. But security guards managed to stop any further fights. When the umpires regained control, they threw out Jackson and Denny.

The game gave Reggie Jackson an opportunity to show the fans why he was a slugger in every sense of the word.

Steve Sax's First Game-winning Homer

July 30, 1985

Steve Sax did more than hurt the opposing team with a clutch homer. He hurt his own coach.

Playing at home in Dodger Stadium against the rival San Francisco Giants, the L.A. second sacker stepped to the plate with a runner on base in the bottom of the ninth inning of a 2–2 game. No one really considered Sax a home run threat because he hadn't hit one out in over a year. But somehow Steve lofted a drive that cleared the wall for a dramatic 4–2 Los Angeles victory.

Because of his inexperience in home run trots, Sax didn't give just an ordinary high-five to Dodgers coach Joe Amalfitano after rounding third base. No, the exuberant Sax delivered a hyperactive hand slap so hard that it broke Amalfitano's thumb.

"I should have known better," said the coach after his thumb was put in a splint. "I saw the crazed look in his eyes when he hit third base."

The following year, when Sax hit his first homer of the 1986 season, he trotted around the bases. But when Sax rounded third base, Amalfitano broke with baseball tradition and refused to shake Sax's hand. Instead, the coach just pointed and pulled an imaginary trigger.

Tim McCarver's Grand Sob

July 4, 1976

On the 200th birthday of the United States of America, Tim McCarver reminded us that we are endowed by our Creator with certain unalienable rights—including the right to screw up.

As a catcher for the Philadelphia Phillies, McCarver hit a grand-slam homer that, because of his boneheaded baserunning, turned into an outside-the-park single.

It happened in the second inning of a game against the Pirates in Pittsburgh. With the bases loaded, McCarver stroked a high, deep drive to right center, and as he ran toward first, he kept his eye on the sailing ball.

Tim failed to notice that Garry Maddox, the runner on first, had retreated to the bag to tag up just in case the ball was caught. As soon as McCarver saw the ball clear the 375-foot sign for a grand slammer, he proudly went into his home run trot with his head down.

After rounding first, McCarver took about four strides before realizing he had passed Maddox on the base path. Tim quickly tried to backpedal but umpire Ed Vargo called, "You're out!" McCarver pleaded, "Oh, no, Ed. I didn't pass him, honest." Vargo smiled and said, "Oh, yes you did."

McCarver, who was credited with a single and three RBIs, walked back to the dugout, hanging his head in shame. Turning to manager Danny Ozark, who was glaring at him, Tim complained, "Geez, how can I become a hero when I keep screwing up?" The stern-faced skipper broke up laughing and so did the rest of the team. After the game (won by the Phillies 10–5), relief pitcher Tug McGraw told McCarver, "That hit of yours deserves a special name. Let's call it 'The Grand Sob.'"

Recalled McCarver, "Hey, what could I do except laugh about it? I mean, when you screw up right out in front of 30,000 people, it's kinda tough to hide. Besides, how can you dig a hole in artificial turf?

"Anyway, it's definitely the longest single I've ever hit. After I hit it, I knew it was gone and I went into my Cadillac trot, head down. The first time I noticed Garry was when I was even with him and Vargo called me out. I guess the moral of the story is to hit 'em so they get out of the park quicker.

"I had a fair idea it wasn't my day when I came up the second time and I looked down and saw that my fly was open."

Tom McCraw's 140-Foot Homer

May 17, 1971

Washington Senators right fielder Tom McCraw lofted a lazy pop fly in short left center. It should have been a simple out. Instead it became an inside-the-park home run—perhaps the cheapest, shortest, and most painful ever hit.

In the fourth inning of a game against the visiting Cleveland Indians, McCraw slapped a soft pop-up beyond the infield. Shortstop Jack Heidemann backpedaled and yelled, "Mine! Mine!" Center fielder Vada Pinson charged in and shouted, "No, I'll take it!" Then left fielder John Lowenstein decided to get into the act. He tried to wave them both off the ball and called out, "I've got it!"

UPI/Bettmann Newsphotos

They all got it—in the head, in the chops, and in the leg—in a bone-crunching collision that triggered a collective gasp throughout RFK Stadium. The impact flipped Heidemann over Lowenstein and into the path of the onrushing Pinson. The trio lay sprawled in the grass looking like the victims of an Indian massacre. The ball, which fell untouched, rolled to a stop just a few feet from the carnage, but the three players were too hurt and dazed to get up and retrieve it.

Meanwhile, McCraw tore around the bases as second sacker Eddie Leon raced out, picked up the ball, and threw it to the plate. But it was too late. McCraw slid home safely for a freak inside-the-park homer.

Players, trainers, and a doctor then dashed to the aid of the injured players. Lowenstein and Heidemann were taken off the field on stretchers while Pinson staggered to the dressing room under his own power. He was given nine stitches to close a wound on his face. The other two were taken to the hospital where Heidemann was treated for a concussion and Lowenstein was treated for a leg injury.

"That was no ball McCraw hit," Lowenstein said later. "That was a bomb."

Babe Ruth's 56th Homer

September 22, 1927

Babe Ruth had an easier time hitting his 56th home run of 1927 than he did circling the bases.

In a thrilling game against the Detroit Tigers at Yankee Stadium, Ruth stepped to the plate in the bottom of the ninth inning. New York was trailing 7–6 with the tying run on first and no outs.

In the seats behind first, a freckle-faced youngster in knickerbockers pleaded at the top of his lungs for Babe to get a hit. Ruth, who had gone hitless in four previous plate appearances, couldn't help but hear the kid, who had been imploring him to do something all afternoon.

With the stage set, the tension high, and the youngster on tenterhooks, the Babe belted a booming drive that chipped a piece out of a seat six rows from the top of the right-field bleachers. It was a dramatic game-winning two-run homer.

Ruth, who decided to carry his bat with him, went into his famous home run trot. When Babe rounded first base, the ecstatic young fan leaped out of his seat, cut across the diamond, and caught up with the slugger near third.

Flailing away with both hands, the deliriously happy boy pounded Babe on the back—and then tried to swipe his bat. But Ruth wasn't about to let go of his cherished piece of lumber. Instead, he gripped the bat handle tighter and continued toward home plate. However, the kid wouldn't give up his hold on the bat either, creating one of the most bizarre scenes ever witnessed on a home run trot. Ruth had to lug the boy across home plate.

As *The New York Times* reported the next day, "The youngster was like the tail of a flying comet, holding onto the bat for dear life and being dragged into the dugout by the Babe."

Cap Anson's Inside-the-Doghouse Home Run

July, 1892

If ever there was a four-bag travesty, this was it.

Cap Anson hit a round-tripper that was so outrageous even the fans who witnessed it didn't believe what they saw.

It happened at Huntington Grounds, where Philadelphia was playing host to Chicago. That stadium had one unique characteristic—a "doghouse." It was a tiny structure with an oval-topped doorway that looked like it had been built for man's best friend. The doghouse was situated at the base of the flagpole in right field and was used to store numbers for the scoreboard.

Even though it was in fair territory, no one had ever paid any attention to the doghouse until the top of the eighth inning in this particular game. Chicago first baseman Cap Anson stepped to the plate with two runners on base and his team trailing 2–1. It was a tense moment. On the first pitch, Anson drilled a high drive that hit the right-field flagpole and dropped straight down into the narrow space between the doghouse and the outfield fence.

Right fielder Ed Delahanty quickly draped himself over the roof of the little house and tried to recover the ball, but failed. In desperation, he dropped to his knees and crawled partway through the narrow door of the doghouse to get at the ball. But then he remembered why he was nicknamed Big Ed. Delahanty couldn't squeeze any more of his body through the opening and he couldn't back out. Big Ed was stuck in the doghouse!

"From the grandstand, all that was visible was the rear elevation of his county seat," wrote Dr. W. N. Pringle, a spectator whose account of the incredible incident was published sixteen years later. "His heels [were] kicking in the air in a lively manner in his frantic efforts to extricate himself.

"In the meantime, Mr. Anson was clearing the bases at a lively clip amid the greatest excitement I ever saw on a ball field. I do not think there were a dozen people in that immense crowd who were not on their feet, laughing, cheering, and yelling themselves hoarse, and throwing hats, canes, and umbrellas in the air."

By the time center fielder Sam Thompson yanked Delahanty free, Anson had crossed home plate with a three-run, inside-the-doghouse home run!

Welcome to the Bigs!

Aspiring major leaguers dream about what that glorious first day in the bigs will be like. They see themselves hammering the winning homer with two out in the bottom of the ninth, or leaping high against the fence to make a game-saving catch. That's the fantasy. The reality is that in their diamond debuts, they often stumble over their feet, fall flat on their faces, or otherwise disgrace themselves so badly that they carry a stigma with them the rest of their careers—which can be a whole lot shorter than they'd planned. For "The Most Inauspicious Major League Debuts," The Baseball Hall of SHAME inducts the following:

Dale Murphy

Catcher • Atlanta, N.L. • 1976

Dale Murphy, All-Star center fielder and two-time National League MVP, literally threw away his career as a catcher.

In 1976, two years after the Atlanta Braves made him their No. 1 draft pick, Murphy was being touted as the next Johnny Bench. He had a live bat and a rifle arm.

But mystifyingly, Dale developed a mental block about throwing to second base. He simply could not make an accurate peg. The strength was there, the concentration was there, the attitude was there. But the ball went nowhere near second. About half the time it went sailing into center field, prompting Murphy's father to tell him. "One thing's for sure, Dale. Nobody will be stealing center field on you."

Murphy's throws wound up decking his own pitchers so often that they began diving to the turf whenever he rose from his crouch. Even that was no safeguard. "One of my most embarrassing moments came on opening night in Richmond when I was still in Triple A," Murphy recalled. "I tried to throw out a runner at second and I hit my own pitcher in the butt—while he was sprawled out on the grass.

"It happened more than once, that's for sure. It seemed like the harder I tried, the worse it got. Some of my pitchers started getting a little shell-shocked. To their credit, they were patient with me. No one really yelled at me. I think they were afraid if they did, I'd start dropping their pitches. At least I could still catch. It was just that I couldn't throw the ball where I wanted. That should have told the Braves something about my major league potential."

Brought up from the minors in 1976, Murphy looked like a can't-miss phenom who missed. When he flopped as a catcher, the Braves made him a first baseman, but he couldn't make throws from there either. So at the start of the 1980 season, manager Bobby Cox sent Murphy to the outfield—and inexplicably his throwing phobia disappeared, just like that.

Today, Murphy is considered among the best center fielders in the game. Looking back on his throwing troubles as a rookie catcher, Murphy says good-naturedly, "I think they put me in center field because it's as far away from home plate as possible."

Warren Spahn

Pitcher • Boston, N.L. • April 20, 1942

As a rookie, Warren Spahn lasted only two games before he was shipped back to the minors—because he failed to hit a batter with a pitch.

Casey Stengel, then the manager of the Boston Braves (one of the league's lousiest teams at the time), brought in Spahn to relieve in a game against the Brooklyn Dodgers. Casey was angry that afternoon because the Dodgers were stealing his team's signs, and he was determined to discourage this thievery. So he ordered Spahn to hit the next batter, Pee Wee Reese.

"When I threw my first pitch, the ball sailed behind Pee Wee and missed him," Spahn recalled. "He knew what was going on, but because I was a fresh rookie, he just laughed at me. Casey signaled me to throw at Reese again and this time I aimed for his chin. But Pee Wee pulled away. I threw all sorts of balls, but I just couldn't hit him."

When the rookie southpaw returned to the dugout after the inning, Stengel was furious. "He cursed me out," said Spahn. "He said I had to learn better control if I ever expected to make it in the majors. The next day he sent me to Hartford of the Eastern League.

"He sent me down because I couldn't hit the batter."

Fortunately, Spahn didn't let his inauspicious debut affect him. He returned from the minors and World War II to become the greatest left-handed pitcher in baseball. He won more games, pitched more innings, hurled more shutouts, and piled up more 20-win seasons than any other southpaw in major league history.

Years after Spahn's debut, Casey Stengel confessed, "Letting go of Spahn was the biggest mistake of my life."

Willie Mays

Outfielder • New York–San Francisco, N.L. • 1951

When Willie Mays first broke into the bigs, he astounded fans right from the start—but not necessarily with the amazing catches and daring baserunning that made him one of the game's greatest players.

Making his debut on May 25, 1951, the highly touted New York Giants rookie was expected to help the team with his hot bat, having hit for a sizzling .477 average in the minors. Willie responded to the challenge. He was called out on strikes in his first at-bat and went 0–for–5 in the game against the Philadelphia Phillies. In the ninth inning, Mays capped off his inauspicious debut by running into right fielder Monte Irvin, causing Irvin to muff a fly ball that fell for a double.

Willie could have used a catcher's mask and helmet in center field in a game against the Chicago Cubs on August 1. When Eddie Miksis hit a line drive to center, Mays was off and running with the crack of the bat. But Willie made a slight miscalculation. The ball caromed off his head for a double. Miksis later scored in the inning and the Cubs went on to win 3–2.

Giants fans didn't know whether to laugh or cry over Willie's baserunning. On June 22 at Wrigley Field, Mays seemed more concerned about looking like a major leaguer than playing like one. When he rounded first base after rapping a single, his cap flew off. So Willie promptly stopped, casually picked up his hat, and then had to make a mad dive back to first, beating the throw-in by an eyelash.

Four days later, in a game against the Brooklyn Dodgers, Mays displayed some classic heads-down baserunning. He followed Alvin Dark's single with a tremendous clout to left center that was just beyond the outfielder's reach. In his haste around the bases, Willie failed to note that Dark had hesitated to make certain the ball wouldn't be caught. As a result, when Dark pulled up at third, Mays was already past second and steaming for third. Dark was forced to break for home and was thrown out by a mile.

The following month, on July 29, Mays stole his first base in a game against the Cincinnati Reds. But Willie didn't have a chance to enjoy the moment. On the very next pitch, he was picked off second by pitcher Willie Ramsdell.

Mays committed another base-path boner on September 3 in the first game of a doubleheader against the Phillies. Mays slammed what appeared to be a two-run, inside-the-park homer. But third baseman Tommy Brown called for the ball, stepped on the bag, and claimed that Willie had missed the base on his turn for home. The umpires agreed and called Mays out. Willie was credited with a double.

"I've heard it said that I sparked the ball club in 1951 because I had a great quality of 'innocence,' " Mays wrote in his autobiography. " 'Ignorance' might be just as good a word for it."

Tommy Lasorda

Pitcher • Brooklyn, N.L. • May 5, 1955

As a rookie pitcher, Tommy Lasorda made such a lasting impression in his first major league start that his team wanted to retire his uniform—with him still in it.

Long before Lasorda became manager of the Los Angeles Dodgers, Tommy tried to break into the bigs as a left-handed pitcher for Brooklyn. His first chance to make the team came in spring training in 1954 when, in a cocky voice, he announced, "I don't intend to let anyone push me off this club, regardless of the record he has." That was a rather brash statement, considering that the Dodgers pitching staff included Preacher Roe, Don Newcombe, Billy Loes, Carl Erskine, Johnny Podres, and Clem Labine. Lasorda didn't even make the team that year.

The following year, Tommy finally got an opportunity to start a major league game. He lasted only one inning, but at least he made it into the record book—for wildness.

In the first inning against the St. Louis Cardinals at Ebbets Field, Lasorda discovered his best friend—the backstop. He unleashed three wild pitches in the inning to tie a then league record.

Shaking enough to make a jackhammer seem calm, the nervous rookie walked leadoff batter Wally Moon. Tommy then threw a wild pitch before walking the next batter, Bill Virdon. With mighty Stan Musial at bat, Lasorda uncorked two *more* wild pitches, the second allowing Moon to slide across the plate with the first run of the game.

On the play, Tommy raced home to cover the plate and was bowled over by Moon. Lasorda recovered to strike out Musial and Rip Repulski before coaxing the next batter into a groundout. Tommy limped back to the dugout where the trainer peeled off the hurler's sock to disclose a spike wound, a painful memento of the play at the plate.

Manager Walter Alston lifted Tommy from the game. Lasorda, a fringe pitcher fighting for a job, pleaded to stay in because the roster-cutting deadline was fast approaching. He didn't want to leave a game in which he had fired three wild pitches after only one inning of work.

Tommy never did win a game in the bigs. In his brief three-year stint, he started six games, had an ERA of 6.48, and finished with an 0–4 record.

Shortly after his debut, the bonus rules of the day forced Brooklyn to keep another wild young southpaw named Sandy Koufax and send Lasorda back to the minors. "Koufax," Tommy snorted. "He'll never amount to much."

Phenomenal Smith

Pitcher • Brooklyn, A.A. • June 17, 1885

For sheer shame, nothing will ever match Phenomenal Smith's pitching debut with Brooklyn. He was slaughtered 18–5 in a scandalous loss that was—yet wasn't—his fault.

The utter disgrace of this game cannot be fully understood by reading the box score, which shows that of the 18 runs scored against him, not a single one was earned.

The seed of ignobility was planted by Smith himself. The twenty-year-old left-handed rookie possessed an enormous ego and gave himself the nickname Phenomenal after hurling a no-hitter for Newark of the Eastern League. When he joined Brooklyn (then in the American Association), the cocky pitcher told his new club that he was so good that he didn't even need them to win. Such brashness did not endear him to his teammates. In fact, they downright hated him. And they took him up on his boast that he could win without their support.

Making his debut for Brooklyn against the visiting St. Louis Cardinals, Phenomenal quickly discovered that his team made no effort to conceal their antipathy toward him on the field. They were determined not only to see him lose, but to see him lose big. Other than third baseman Bill McClellan, who played to win despite his dislike for Smith, the infielders intentionally dropped pop-ups, let grounders skip through their legs, and threw wildly as they racked up 14 errors. Their misplays were so blatant that the players were roundly booed by the 1,600 disgusted spectators at Washington Park.

The next day, the *Brooklyn Eagle* condemned "the disgusting rottenness which prevailed in the ranks of the team." The paper blasted the conspirators for not having "brains enough to properly conceal their little game." The *Eagle* declared, "They so plainly exposed their hands in their crooked work that the occupants of the grandstand saw it, and it aroused their just indignation to such an extent that they hissed the wretched muffing work of the [Brooklyn players]."

Germany Smith was the most flagrant fumbler, committing seven errors at shortstop, while co-conspirator and catcher Jackie Hayes made two miscues and was charged with five passed balls. The official box score doesn't reflect the easy fly balls and grounders that the Brooklyn fielders let go untouched for base hits.

"It's an outrage!" stormed Charles Byrne, president of the Brooklyn club, after the debacle. "The way my men treat this new player is a disgrace, and I will take steps to punish them for it." He did, too, fining each of the guilty players $500. But to the delight of the club, Byrne reluctantly released Phenomenal. It was the only way Byrne could ensure team harmony.

Larry Monroe

Pitcher • Chicago, A.L. • September 14, 1976

When Chicago White Sox manager Paul Richards announced that Larry Monroe would pitch against the division-leading Kansas City Royals in his first major league start, the rookie was thrilled and honored.

He wouldn't have been had he known the cruel truth.

"At the time, Kansas City had a three-game lead in our division, so when I was told I'd start, I figured that Richards had faith in me," recalled Monroe. "I felt that my debut against the Royals would show everybody that I was good enough to start against the best in the league.

"I was really pumped up. I left passes at the gate for about fifty relatives and friends so they could watch my debut as a starter."

The young right-hander didn't do badly. He gave up a run in the first inning on a George Brett triple, but settled down in the next frame. Monroe's worst moment came when he returned to the dugout after the second inning and heard Richards say, "That's it, son. You're done. I'm bringing in a lefty."

Monroe couldn't believe what he was hearing. "Why are you doing this?" he demanded.

"I just wanted them to start their left-handed lineup," Richards replied smugly.

Monroe angrily slammed his hat and glove against the dugout floor and stormed off into the clubhouse. What should have been the most exciting moment of his playing career was nothing more than a ploy hatched by Richards. The manager never had any intention of letting Monroe pitch more than a couple of innings. Once Monroe had faced everyone in the Royals' lefty-loaded batting order, Richards brought in southpaw Terry Forster, hoping to get the edge on the Kansas City hitters. The scheme backfired. Forster went on to lose his eleventh game of the season.

"Richards just used me in front of my family and friends," recalled a still-bitter Monroe. "Before I could even get my feet on the ground, he jerked me out. It was a hell of a cynical thing for him to do. I think he should have been honest with me. It was a terrible blow to me."

It didn't help matters any when Richards cracked an insensitive joke at Monroe's expense after the game. When reporters asked Richards why he yanked the rookie so soon, the manager quipped, "I just didn't want to send him back out there again. George Brett and John Mayberry might have killed him the second time around."

Although Monroe didn't figure in the decision, he was still a loser. "When Richards pulled me from that game, I had a lot of bad things to say about him in the Chicago press," Monroe said. "After that, he ignored me. He put me in a few games in relief just to mop up. That was the end of my major league career." Monroe pitched only 22 innings that year and never played again in the majors.

Ted Williams

Outfielder • Boston, A.L. • April 1, 1939

When Ted Williams made the Boston Red Sox, the rookie showed he could drive the ball out of sight—and drive manager Joe Cronin out of his mind.

Williams got into hot water with Cronin even before the temperamental outfielder had played in his first official game. It happened when Ted lost his cool during a spring training game against the Cincinnati Reds in Atlanta.

In the ninth inning, Williams ran after a long fly ball that drifted into foul territory. He camped under the ball, but it bounced out of his glove. Ted angrily picked up the ball, unintentionally dropped it, then clumsily booted it as he reached down for it. Seething mad, Williams finally grabbed hold of the ball and flung it over the grandstand roof. The ball bounced off a Sears store across the street.

Cronin immediately called time and yanked the hotheaded rookie from the game. That night, the veteran player-manager engaged in an earnest fatherly talk. "Explain something to me," Cronin said to Williams. "Here I've worked all my life to make myself a big leaguer, and a kid like you comes along with all the natural ability anybody could hope to have and behaves like you did out there today. I just can't understand it." Unable to defend his actions, Ted hung his head in shame.

But the talk didn't seem to make much of an impression on the brash twenty-year-old. More than once during his first few months in the majors, Williams loafed in the outfield. He heard about it, too. At the end of the inning, Cronin, waiting at his shortstop position, would bawl Ted out all the way into the dugout.

Williams tended to take a rather cavalier attitude toward ground balls when he first came up to the majors. He preferred hitting more than fielding. As a result, whenever there was a crucial moment in the game, Cronin would look over his shoulder to make sure his newest outfielder was ready. Once in a tight game, Cronin saw Ted in the outfield taking practice swings at imaginary balls. So the manager called time and, mimicking Williams's swings, yelled at him, "Hey, Bush, never mind practicing *this* ..." Then, going through the motions of scooping up imaginary ground balls, Cronin shouted at him, "Practice *this*!"

Sick's Seattle Stadium

1969

Sick's Seattle Stadium—home of the American League's short-lived expansion team, the Pilots—couldn't have been more appropriately named.

Fans had to endure toiling construction workers, bleacher splinters, backed-up toilets, faulty portable johns, and waterless faucets.

In order to bring the minor league park up to major league standards, the city promised to have the stadium enlarged by the time the Pilots played their home opener on April 11, 1969. However, remodeling Sick's didn't begin until just three months before the start of the season. That wasn't nearly enough time to get finished. Three weeks before the first game, only 7,500 seats were ready. Complained the club's president, Dewey Soriano, "People come here and want to buy tickets and I can't even show them where they're going to sit."

While the Pilots were winners of their home opener, the ball park was definitely a loser. Instead of the promised 25,000 seats by Opening Day, only 18,000 were ready. About 200 hard-hat-wearing construction workers were still putting up bleachers, painting, drilling, and installing seats as the fans crammed into the park. Ticket manager Harry McCarthy was forced to ask 700 early-arriving ticket holders to wait an hour before the game until carpenters could put the finishing touches on their seats. Hundreds of other spectators didn't bother with tickets. They enjoyed a free view of the game by looking through the numerous openings in the unfinished left-field fence.

"The work was done so poorly and so quickly in order to get ready to open that they had to use wooden planks for the bleacher seats and this caused numerous problems," recalled Bill Sears, public relations director of the club. "On Opening Day, one guy showed us the seat of his pants. It had been torn by the splinters on the bleachers. There were many times from then on that we had to buy people new clothing. We also had a first-aid station set up specifically to treat cases of splinters in the butt. The spectators out there were damn unhappy."

To make matters worse, Sick's Stadium suffered from a severe plumbing problem that affected both the players and the fans. "When they enlarged the park, they forgot to take into consideration the need to improve the plumbing to handle the bigger crowds," said Sears. If attendance climbed above 14,000, the water pressure fell to almost nothing. "Sometimes both teams couldn't take showers after the game because there was no water," said Sears. "When this happened, the visiting team had to go back to the hotel to shower while the Pilots went home to wash.

"The fans were always complaining that the plumbing in the rest rooms didn't work well at all. When people flushed the toilets all over the stadium, the water pressure would go way down. Not enough water came out of the faucets in the concession stands to even make coffee. You couldn't flush the toilets up in the press box until about the seventh inning because there just wasn't enough water pressure. So from the first day on, we started a tradition up there called the 'Seventh Inning Flush.'"

In a valiant attempt to alleviate the problem, portable johns were set up in the bleacher areas. Unfortunately, they proved too popular—the toilets backed up. That was the least concern of one poor soul. Somehow, he accidentally got locked in one of the portable toilets and spent the night trapped inside. "When the cleanup crew arrived the next morning, they heard this guy pounding on the door, so they unlocked the door and he took off on a dead run," said Sears. "We never did find out who he was. God only knows what kind of an excuse he gave his wife when he got home."

Joe "Fire" Cleary

Pitcher • Washington, A.L. • August 4, 1945

Joe Cleary was determined to leave his mark in his major league debut. And he did—a black one.

Appearing on the mound for the first time, Cleary faced nine batters and managed to get only one out. He gave up seven earned runs on five hits and three walks before he was given the hook.

Joe never pitched again. But to this day, he still holds a record—for the highest lifetime ERA in the bigs. It's an astronomical 189.00! That works out to 21 earned runs an inning.

Cleary started out in organized baseball as a second baseman but switched to pitching because, he once explained, "I got disgusted with our pitchers, who could hardly get a man out." After his major league debut, he realized he had spoken too soon.

After bouncing around in the minors for four years, the Irish-born hurler got his chance to pitch in the bigs when the Washington Senators signed him on August 3, 1945. The next day, Joe was called on to relieve starter Sandy Ullrich, who was knocked out of the box by the Boston Red Sox in the top of the fourth inning.

Cleary took the mound with his team trailing 6–2. Boston already had scored four runs in the inning and had a runner perched on third. The Red Sox bats were smoking now, and rather than put out the blaze, Joe merely fanned the flames. (Perhaps that's how he got the nickname "Fire.") He never did finish the inning. He faced everyone in the Boston lineup once and got only one out—he fanned opposing pitcher Boo Ferriss. As a result, Ferriss holds the dubious distinction of being the only player who ever failed to reach base against the pitcher with the worst ERA in history.

Cleary was yanked from the mound with the bases loaded and two outs and Boston ahead 14–2. He walked off the field and never returned.

In to relieve him went Bert Shepard, who, ironically, was another hurler making his first and last appearance in a major league game. Shepard pitched superbly, giving up one run on three hits in 5⅓ innings. What made Shepard's stats so amazing was that he had only one leg. He played on an artificial limb. Despite his good showing, the Senators released him and no other major league team wanted a disabled player, no matter how good he was.

At least Joe Cleary's abysmal one-shot performance had a good side. "If Cleary hadn't done so poorly, I might never have had the chance to pitch in the major leagues, even if it was for only one game," said Shepard. "I have to thank him for that."

THE FALL FOLLIES

The World Series isn't always all that it's cracked up to be. Naturally, the lords of baseball want everyone to believe that the October extravaganza showcases the leagues' two best teams with brilliant fielding, thrilling baserunning, dynamite hitting, and awesome pitching. In truth, the Fall Classic is often the Classic Fall from grace to disgrace for so-called champions. For The Most Atrocious World Series Performances," "The Baseball Hall of SHAME inducts the following:

St. Louis Cardinals

October 26–27, 1985

The St. Louis Cardinals lost more than just the 1985 World Series. They lost their heads, their dignity—and the respect of millions of baseball fans.

St. Louis seemingly had the Series all wrapped up. The year's winningest team held a commanding 3-games-to-1 edge over the Kansas City Royals. But after losing Game 5, the Cards contracted a terminal case of petulance during the last two contests.

And when they lost it all in the final game, they blamed an umpire's bad call in the ninth inning of Game 6 for costing them the Series. There was no doubt that the ump made a horrible error. But the man in blue didn't cause the Cardinals to score only a pitiful 13 runs in seven games, hit for a low .185 team batting average, or fail to make the crucial but easy plays in the pinch.

For most of the Series, fans admired the Cards' nifty pitching and clutch hitting. Then came the pivotal Game 6 at Royals Stadium. Entering the bottom of the ninth nursing a 1–0 lead, St. Louis seemed certain to become the world champs. The team couldn't wait to break open the cases of bubbly that were stashed on ice in their clubhouse. The Cards, who hadn't blown a ninth-inning lead all season, needed only three more outs to win the World Series.

Kansas City pinch hitter Jorge Orta led off the ninth with an easy grounder to first baseman Jack Clark. Clark flipped the ball to pitcher Todd Worrell, who was racing over to cover first for the apparent out. But in one of the most atrociously blown calls ever made in the Fall Classic, umpire Don Denkinger called Orta safe. TV replays clearly show that Orta's foot was about six inches from the base when Worrell stepped on the bag with the ball in his glove.

Livid Cardinals manager Whitey Herzog roared out of the dugout and vociferously protested the call. He lost both the argument and his voice. Still, championship teams manage to overcome mistakes like this. But the Cardinals chose to dwell on it instead. Fleeced out of a putout, the team began to self-destruct.

On the next pitch, Steve Balboni lofted a stratospheric pop-up near the Royals' dugout. Clark drifted under the catchable ball, but looked first at catcher Darrell Porter, then at the dugout, and finally at the ball as it dropped untouched behind him. The Royals should have been down to their final out. Two pitches later, Balboni singled.

Following a force-out at third, the stage was set for another Cardinal defensive lapse that unraveled the entire game. With pinch hitter Hal McRae at bat, Worrell threw a "crossed-up" pitch—a hard slider that should have been a fastball—that Porter failed to block. The runners advanced to second and third. Using traditional strategy, St. Louis walked McRae to load the bases. But fate was smiling on the Royals, and pinch hitter Dane Iorg dumped a broken-bat single into right field to win the game for Kansas City, 2–1.

Herzog took the loss with the grace of a true gentleman—one who overdosed on pugnacity. "It's bleeping unbelievable," he groused. "We're gonna win the bleeping World Series and he [Denkinger] boots that play."

Taking their cue from Herzog, the people in St. Louis demanded the umpire's scalp. The *St. Louis Post-Dispatch* fanned the flames by calling Denkinger "Jesse James" as if no umpire in World Series history had ever missed one before. A St. Louis disc jockey gave out Denkinger's home phone number and address so fans could harass him in the off-season. "Maybe we shouldn't even show up for Game 7," griped Herzog. "Maybe we won't." It seemed pretty obvious that the cork would pop on something other than a champagne bottle in the Cardinals' clubhouse after the final game.

Kansas City routed St. Louis 11–0 for the World Championship. The Redbirds did not go gently into the night. St. Louis' starting pitcher John Tudor was so upset by his shabby 2⅓ innings (five earned runs and four walks) that he took a poke at an electrical fan in the clubhouse and had to be taken to the hospital to treat his cut hand. But that wasn't the big story.

The Cards' anger and frustration boiled over, disgracing the game with an ugly, deplorable scene in the fifth inning.

With the score 9–0, Herzog—for reasons known only to him—called on Joaquin Andujar, the human time bomb, to relieve. Andujar was still smoking over the blown call the night before by Denkinger, who had moved behind the plate for the final game. When Denkinger called an obviously wide pitch a ball, Andujar flew into one of his patented tantrums. Herzog rushed out to restrain him and ended up verbally lashing out at Denkinger. "We shouldn't even be out here tonight!" Herzog bellowed at the umpire. "You know you blew that call!" Denkinger ejected him. The irate manager didn't seem to mind. "I've seen enough anyway," he snarled.

Herzog's tirade had lit the fuse under his explosive pitcher. The next pitch by Andujar was also an apparent ball, but the sorehead was determined to pick another fight with the umpire and he, too, was tossed out. It was the first time both a manager and a player had been ejected from a Series game in fifty years. "I'm not sorry for nothing!" Andujar snapped. He had to be wrestled away by teammates who must have finally realized that all Cardinal class was rapidly vaporizing into the cool Missouri night. Even commissioner Peter Ueberroth squirmed in his seat. "Personally, I was disappointed," said Ueberroth, who later suspended Andujar for the first ten days of the 1986 season. "All I could do was sit there. I was just hoping it would go away."

Finally, it did. But the stigma of the Cardinals' sorry display of poor sportsmanship will always remain.

St. Louis Browns

Never in World Series history has a team displayed such amazing incompetence on one seemingly simple play.

The St. Louis Browns turned red from embarrassment by handling the ball as if they had never touched one before. With a flair for botchery seldom seen in any Little League game, let alone a championship contest, the Browns dropped, kicked, fumbled, and threw away the ball *six* times while trying to field a puny twenty-foot bunt.

The debacle occurred in the bottom of the third inning of Game 2 of the 1944 Series clash between the Browns and their crosstown rival Cardinals.

The game was scoreless when Emil Verban led off the inning for the Cards with a base hit. Everyone in the ball park knew that the next batter, pitcher Max Lanier, would attempt to lay down a sacrifice bunt. The Browns appeared ready; the fielders at first and third would charge the plate and the second baseman would cover first.

As expected, Lanier squared away and bunted. It was a little pop-up between the mound and home on the third-base side of the diamond. Catcher Red Hayworth broke from the plate, Mark Christman charged in from third, and pitcher Nelson Potter moved in from the mound. But then all three stopped as if someone had yelled, "Freeze!" The trio stared at each other and then at the ball, which by this time had plopped safely to the ground. That was Misplay No. 1.

Potter still had a chance to nail Lanier at first, but when he tried to field the ball, he bobbled it for Misplay No. 2. Unwilling to give up, Potter finally found the handle, but then fired the ball wildly to first base. It sailed over the head of second baseman Don Gutteridge, who was covering first on the play, for Misplay No. 3.

The ball rolled down the right-field line, where outfielder Gene Moore joined the act with some funny fielding of his own. As Moore bent down to pick up the ball, it rolled through his legs for Misplay No. 4. For an encore, he picked up the ball and dropped it. That was Misplay No. 5. Totally frustrated and desperate, Moore heaved the ball over Gutteridge's head for Misplay No. 6, the final joke in the Browns' comedy routine.

The official scorer, who couldn't believe his eyes, benevolently charged the Browns with only two errors on the play, which had put runners Lanier and Verban on first and third, respectively. On the next play, an infield out, Verban scored an unearned run and the Cardinals went on to beat the error-plagued Browns, 3–2.

Lou Brock

Outfielder • St. Louis, N.L. • October 7, 1968

Lou Brock—considered one of the game's greatest base runners—waited until the 1968 World Series to pull the biggest boneheaded play of his record-breaking career.

It was his smart running that helped lead the St. Louis Cardinals to the Series. But it was his foolish base-path miscalculation that turned the tide against the Cards, enabling the Detroit Tigers to win the Fall Classic.

St. Louis had won three of the first four games and led 3–2 in Game 5 when Brock doubled in the fifth inning. Julian Javier then singled to left field and Brock streaked around third and headed for home.

Meanwhile, left fielder Willie Horton charged the ball, fielded it cleanly, and fired it to catcher Bill Freehan. Everyone in the ball park expected a close play at the plate. And everyone expected Brock to slide. It just made

good baseball sense because he had no chance of bowling over the burly Freehan and he couldn't afford to take a chance with a fragile one-run lead.

Incredibly, rather than hitting the dirt, Brock came in standing up. The baserunning gaffe allowed Freehan an additional split second to catch Horton's throw, block the plate, and put an easy tag on Brock. TV replays and photos clearly show that the speedster certainly would have scored if he had slid. The Cardinals would have boosted their lead to 4–2 and perhaps kept the inning alive with more runs. In fact, St. Louis could have wrapped up the Series then and there.

Instead, Brock's goof proved to be the turning point of the whole Series. The Tigers rallied to win the game, 5–3, then won the next two to capture the World Championship. Although Brock tied a Series record with 13 hits and stole seven bases, his failure to slide made him less of a hero and more of a goat.

Frankie Frisch

Manager • St. Louis, N.L. • October 6, 1934

In the dumbest managerial move in World Series history, Frankie Frisch risked injury to his most valuable player for a task that could have been filled by an unproven rookie.

Frisch took a monumental—and totally unnecessary—gamble by using star pitcher Dizzy Dean as a pinch runner in the fourth inning of Game 4 of the 1934 World Series. The move turned into a near tragedy.

Trailing the Detroit Tigers 4–3, the St. Louis Cardinals had runners on the corners with one out. Suddenly, the crowd went wild. Dizzy Dean, grinning ear to ear in a spotless uniform, went in to pinch-run for Virgil Davis at first base. The crowd thought it was a wonderful lark.

But players, sportswriters, and those in the know were incredulous. Why was Dean—the pitcher who had won 30 games, who led the Cardinals to the pennant, who won his first Series game with only two days' rest—pinch-running? Any utility player could have run. Any benchwarmer, even any other pitcher, could have done the job. But why risk injury to Dizzy—the man whom the Cardinals were depending upon to win the Series for them?

Before second guessers could discuss the move, their worst fears were realized. Pepper Martin rapped a grounder to Charlie Gehringer at second. Gehringer tossed the ball to shortstop Bill Rogell, forcing Dean at second. But even though he was out, Dizzy was determined to break up the double play and came in to second base standing up. Rogell, who was just three feet away, tried to complete the twin killing anyway and whipped a bullet toward first. The ball never found its target. It struck Dean flush on the forehead with such a terrific force that it bounded 30 feet into the air and more than 100 feet into short right field. The impact of the ball against Dizzy's skull made the sound of a car backfiring. He crumpled and fell like a marionette whose strings had snapped.

A hush descended over the 36,000 spectators who feared the worst. The nearly unconscious Dean was carried off the field on a stretcher. When he was revived in the clubhouse, Dizzy appeared to be his old self again. The first thing he said was, "They didn't get Pepper, did they?"

After the game (won by Detroit, 10–4), a still-shaken Frisch explained to the press why he made his dumb move. "Dean kept pulling my sleeve and begging me to use him," the manager said. "I knew that he was a fine runner and that I had used him as such before. I did not think it even remotely possible that he could be injured in such a role, so I consented and let him go."

Dizzy was taken to the hospital for a complete examination. All he suffered was a headache and a big knot on his forehead. He also suffered a ribbing the next day over this newspaper headline: X-RAYS OF DEAN'S HEAD REVEAL NOTHING.

Chicago Cubs—Boston Red Sox

September 10, 1918

In 1918, the United States was fighting "the war to end all wars"; doughboys were sacrificing their lives and limbs; Americans at home were working overtime to support their boys on the fields of battle.

Meanwhile, the Chicago Cubs and Boston Red Sox were so greedy and self-centered they staged a sitdown strike before Game 5 of the World Series. The teams had the audacity during those deeply troubled times to hold out for a bigger share of the World Series pot.

Such inexcusable selfishness had never tainted the Fall Classic before nor has it since.

Because of World War I, the baseball season ended early and the Series began on September 5, 1918. It was hoped that the games would provide Americans a brief respite from the tragedies of war. Instead, the Series reminded people of one of man's basic vices—avarice.

At the end of the first four games, the two teams were disgruntled because so few fans had shown up. Never mind that the country was at war. The upset players realized that the low attendance meant a meager payoff for them, so they demanded that the baseball establishment sweeten the pot. They were turned down.

The Cubs and Red Sox fought back. A few hours before Game 5 at Fenway Park, the players went on strike. They simply refused to play until they were promised a larger share of the World Series receipts. They couldn't have cared less about the 25,000 fans—including thousands of wounded sailors and soldiers—who were waiting for the game to begin, and by this time wondering if it ever would.

Talks with a strike committee of players dragged on and on. Game time came and went as the two owners and several peacemakers pleaded in vain with the players to take to the field. It was only after the crowd began to show impatience by booing and yelling at the stubborn strikers that the players gave up their demand for more money. They finally came to their senses and realized they had a duty to the game and to the public.

After holding up the game for more than an hour, the rebellious players suited up and went out to play. The Cubs won the game, 3–0, but the Red Sox won the Series the following day. However, in the eyes of war-weary Americans, both teams were losers for striking the Fall Classic.

Joaquin Andujar's Post-game Interview

October 20, 1982

When the St. Louis Cardinals won the 1982 World Series, Busch Stadium was awash with waving red pennants—and shocking blue language.

Although the Cards' volcanic pitcher Joaquin Andujar was the cause of the shame, he wasn't to blame. Andujar, a renowned hot dog on the mound, displayed many inflammatory mannerisms, such as forming his hand into a pistol and aiming it at the batter after a strike. Naturally, this tended to tick off opposing players.

So it was nothing unusual when Andujar deliberately irked Milwaukee Brewers second baseman Jim Gantner in the final game of the Series, won by St. Louis, 6–3. With two out in the seventh inning, Gantner hit the ball back to Andujar. To show up the hitter, Andujar held on to the ball just long enough to keep Gantner running to first. After getting thrown out to end the inning, the aggravated Gantner did a quick burn, turned toward the mound, and called Andujar an unspeakable name. Andujar replied that Gantner was an unspeakable unspeakable and that he didn't have to take that kind of unspeakable verbal abuse from anyone. Then the volatile hurler challenged Gantner to fight him. Hearing more than enough, hefty home plate umpire Lee Weyer stepped between the two piqued players and marched Andujar back to the Cardinals' dugout.

After the game, amid the raucous cheers, victory cigars, and champagne spraying, Andujar was asked in the press interview room to recount his earlier cussing duel with Gantner. Andujar thoughtfully asked if he could possibly repeat such off-color language in the microphones. When informed that he could, he cheerfully obliged, making sure not to leave out a single choice swear word.

Incredibly, no one realized that the Cards' post-game interviews were being piped into the stadium's public address system. As a result, Andujar's entire X-rated recitation was broadcast to every corner of the ball park, where thousands of spectators were still celebrating. Did the fans gasp in mortification? Did they cover their ears? Did they hustle their innocent children out of the stadium? Not exactly. After every single foul utterance from Andujar, the fans stood up and cheered.

Red Faber

Pitcher • Chicago, A.L. • October 7, 1917

In the 1917 World Series, Hall of Fame pitcher Red Faber scored his biggest triumph—and committed one of the Fall Classic's biggest baserunning blunders.

As a pitcher for the Chicago White Sox, Faber dominated the New York Giants, beating them three times as the Sox drubbed the Giants, four games to two.

However, as a base runner, Red would have been better off sitting on the bench. That, apparently, was where he left his brains during the fifth inning of Game 2.

With teammate Buck Weaver on first base, Faber drilled a base hit to right field and took second on the throw-in to third. Faber, who collected only four hits during the whole season for an abysmal .058 batting average, was so thrilled with his World Series single that he forgot all about Weaver standing on third.

As the next batter dug in at the plate, Giants pitcher Pol Perritt didn't even bother glancing back to second base. There was no reason to do so. Red was a slow runner, and besides, Weaver was already on third. With two out and two on and the Sox ahead 7–2, Perritt went into a big windup.

Faber, still pumped up by his base hit, figured that even though he was no speed merchant on the base paths, he could surely steal third because Perritt didn't go into a stretch. Red just couldn't resist the temptation and blindly motored to third base, arriving in a dusty slide—and bewilderment.

Much to his astonishment, Faber looked up and saw Weaver peering down at him. "What the hell are you doing here?" Buck demanded. Red, who was tagged out to end the inning, replied, "Why, I'm just going out to pitch, of course."

SNOOZE PLAYS

Major leaguers concentrate on every pitch, every batted ball, every play. Baloney! These guys daydream and get lost in their thoughts just like the rest of us working stiffs. The only problem is that their office is the playing field, and when they get caught napping, they're in for a rude awakening. For "The Most Mind-boggling Mental Miscues," The Baseball Hall of SHAME inducts the following:

Steve Garvey   Ron Cey

First Baseman   Third Baseman
Los Angeles, N.L. • June 12, 1980

For one brief moment, Steve Garvey and Ron Cey looked like the players of the 1930s. That's because the Dodger duo set the game back fifty years.

Garvey and Cey were not playing with a full deck in a game against the Mets in New York. In the seventh inning, with the Dodgers trailing 6-5, Garvey was standing on first base and Cey was at the plate with a 2-2 count.

In came the pitch. A ball. Cey, whose mind must have been wandering in the upper grandstand, thought it was ball four and brainlessly headed for first. Garvey, considered one of the smartest players in the game, compounded the gaffe. Not only did he ignore his own reckoning of the count, but he also carelessly assumed that Cey knew what he was doing. So Garvey started to trot toward second.

At least Mets catcher John Stearns knew the correct count was 3-and-2. He whipped the ball to second and easily nailed Garvey. Meanwhile, the red-faced Cey was called back to the plate. The Dodgers never recovered from the blunder and lost 6-5.

"I've never seen a play like that," said Los Angeles manager Tommy Lasorda, shaking his head in disbelief. "Cey thought he had four balls and then convinced Garvey. It was just bad baseball."

In a classic understatement, Garvey admitted, "It was a little embarrassing. Halfway down the line, I looked at the scoreboard and saw it changed from two balls to three. Then I started to run." But by then it was too late.

The question in the Dodger clubhouse was, who was dumber? Cey, who *couldn't* count to four, or Garvey, who *didn't* count to four?

Lee Lacy

Outfielder • Baltimore, A.L. • June 29, 1986

Lee Lacy took a rest—just long enough for him to look like an oafish lazybones in the outfield. That's because he picked the worst possible moment during the game for his respite—while the ball was still in play.

Lacy was playing right field for the Baltimore Orioles in a home game against the Boston Red Sox. It was a Sunday, and Lacy apparently was observing the day of rest in his own special way.

In the ninth inning of an 8–3 Boston win, Don Baylor slapped a fly ball down the right-field line. Lacy ran a long way but failed to reach the ball, which he assumed had landed in foul territory. Being a major league ball player, Lacy should have known better than to assume anything.

After his lengthy run, he stopped in foul territory, where he draped his arms and elbows over the railing and dropped his head. Oblivious to all around him, he caught his breath—and then he caught hell. Lacy never bothered to check the umpire, who had called the ball fair.

While Baylor was scurrying around the bases, the fans in right field were screaming at Lacy to turn around and chase the ball. By the time he looked up, tracked down the ball, and fired it into the infield, Lacy's mental lapse had stretched Baylor's pop-fly single into a stand-up triple.

Lacy wasn't his normal self after the game. Usually, he talks so much that his teammates ask the clubhouse man for cotton to plug their ears. But this time, he had nothing to say.

Ricky Peters

Pinch Runner • Oakland, A.L. • June 25, 1986

After committing one of the stupidest baserunning gaffes in years, Ricky Peters should have been sent back to kindergarten for a refresher course in counting to four.

He earned an "F" in remedial arithmetic when he incorrectly added up the number of runners on base. Peters somehow thought that two plus one made four. He quickly learned that his figures added up to a mortifying loss.

In a game against the Kansas City Royals, the visiting Oakland A's entered the ninth inning tied 4–4. After Jerry Willard opened the top of the ninth with a single, Peters was put in as a pinch runner. Ricky, who represented the lead run, was then sacrificed to second before Carney Lansford was walked intentionally. The next batter fanned for the second out. With José Canseco at the plate, Royals hurler Steve Farr threw a wild pitch and both runners advanced. Peters was now only ninety feet away with the potential winning run.

The blunder that seemed impossible in the major leagues occurred seconds after Farr walked Canseco. This should have loaded the bases. But incredibly, Peters thought that the bases were *already* loaded and began to trot happily toward home plate. Third base coach Bob Didier couldn't believe his eyes. He shouted, "Back! Back! Back!"

When Peters realized his mistake, he wheeled around, sprinted back toward third, and slid into the base. But it was too late. He was out. The rally was killed. The inning was over. After blowing the game in the top of the ninth, the A's lost it in the bottom of the frame, 5–4.

"Gee," said Farr, the winning pitcher. "That's the first time I've ever gotten out of an inning on a walk."

A's manager Jackie Moore, so livid after the game he could hardly talk, growled, "Ricky thought the bases were loaded. How could he? He had just run to third on a wild pitch. This is the big leagues—and this is embarrassing. The bottom line is we looked like a bunch of idiots. Every night something bad happens. I don't know what the answer is." Apparently the front office did. Moore was fired as manager the next day. Presumably, he should have known better than to count on a pinch runner who couldn't count.

Ted Simmons

Catcher • Milwaukee, A.L. • June 16, 1982

The catcher's mask, chest protector, and shin guards are called the "tools of ignorance." Ted Simmons showed why.

The Milwaukee Brewers were in Baltimore playing the Orioles in a scoreless game when the O's rallied in the bottom of the third, putting runners on first and second with one out.

The next batter, John Lowenstein, struck out. Simmons, stupidly thinking there were three outs, casually flipped the ball to home plate umpire George Maloney and jogged toward the dugout. Maloney instinctively caught the ball and then suddenly dropped it, realizing the ball was still in play.

Before Ted discovered his mistake, runners Dan Ford and Eddie Murray raced to third and second respectively. Trying desperately to hide his shame behind his catcher's mask, Simmons walked back to his position as Joe

Nolan stepped to the plate. Taking full advantage of Ted's snooze play, Nolan laced a single to right, driving in two runs.

Perhaps the boner would have been forgotten if the Brewers had won. But the game ended in a 2–2 tie rather than a 2–1 Milwaukee victory. A downpour forced the umpires to call off the action after nine innings and the game had to be replayed in its entirety. Magnifying the blunder even more, the Brewers and the Orioles were battling neck and neck for the AL East title.

For more than three months—right up until the final day of the season—Simmons had to fret over the sickening thought that he could become the modern-day Fred Merkle. As you no doubt know, Fred Merkle cost the New York Giants a victory over the Chicago Cubs when he forgot to touch second base after a teammate's apparent game-winning hit. Instead of a New York victory, the game ended in a tie. The Giants, forced to replay the contest at season's end, lost the makeup game—and the pennant to the Cubs by one game.

Like the Giants, the Brewers lost their replayed game to the Orioles on the final weekend of the season. The O's went on to win three straight from Milwaukee and tied the Brewers for first place. But on the last day of the season, Milwaukee won to capture the pennant by only a single game over Baltimore.

When asked during the heat of the pennant race if he was aware of the parallel with Merkle, Simmons replied, "I've only thought about it every day since it happened."

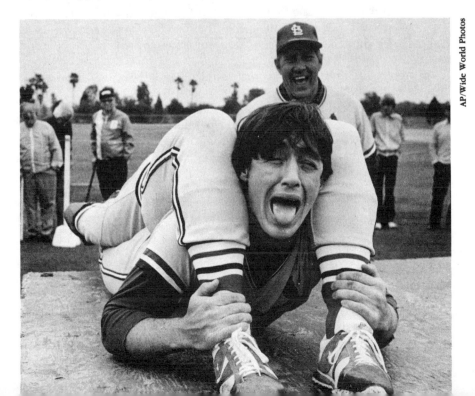

Lenny Randle and the New York Mets

John Kibler and the Umpiring Crew

May 5, 1978

In a classic mass snooze play, an entire team and an umpiring crew fell victim to a bizarre epidemic of forgetfulness. As a result, Lenny Randle owns the distinction of being the first hitter on record ever to triple off a 4–and–2 pitch. That's right, a 4–and–2 pitch.

The unprecedented pitch came in the ninth inning of a game between the visiting New York Mets and the Philadelphia Phillies. With his team ahead 9–4, Philly relief ace Tug McGraw worked the count to 3-and-2 against Mets third baseman Lenny Randle. The next pitch was a high outside fastball.

It should have been ball four. But Randle, who should have known a walk when he saw one—he was leading the league in walks—didn't head to first base. He merely blinked, stepped out of the batter's box, and scooped up a handful of dirt. No one on the Mets, who desperately needed base runners, said a word. That shows you how involved they were in the game.

Meanwhile, umpire John Kibler was puzzled. He looked at the scoreboard and figured he had made a mistake, so he turned back his ball-and-strike indicator to 3–and–2. None of the other umpires spoke up, which shows you how involved they were in the game. The scoreboard operator was just as confused. He thought that he had made the error, so he kept the board at 3–and–2.

Apparently, the only ones who realized that Randle was entitled to a free pass were the Phillies. And they weren't about to say anything.

Ray Rippelmeyer, the Phils pitching coach, figured something was wrong. He was charting the pitches and he had run out of spaces on the paper. Tug McGraw knew exactly what was happening. "I knew it was ball four," he recalled. "But when nobody reacted, I couldn't wait to get the ball back from catcher Bob Boone. I got right back on the rubber and threw another fastball."

Too bad McGraw wasn't more honest. He would have been better off clueing in Randle and the ump to the correct count. On his 4– and–2 pitch, Randle drilled the ball to left field for a triple. That ended a string in which Tug had retired thirty-five consecutive Mets during the past two seasons. Undismayed, McGraw began a new streak by retiring the next three batters and stranding Randle at third.

Phillies manager Danny Ozark said he deliberately kept mum on the count. "If Randle didn't want to take a base on balls, it was okay by me," he said. "Then after he hit a triple, there was nothing I could do about it. I would have looked silly going out and asking the umpires to send him back to first base."

Maybe so. But Ozark wouldn't have looked any sillier than Randle and the rest of the Mets . . . or Kibler and the rest of the umpiring crew.

Doc Semmens

Trainer • Cincinnati, N.L. • April 29, 1913

When the Cincinnati Reds boarded the train in St. Louis for the trip to Chicago, team trainer Doc Semmens was in charge of the Reds' baggage. He checked the players' personal luggage, the equipment trunks, and the training room supplies. He didn't leave anything behind—except the uniforms.

Not until the team arrived in Chicago did the absentminded trainer realize he had forgotten to load the trunks containing all the uniforms. They were still sitting on the platform at the train station back in St. Louis. With all the courage he could muster, he told his bosses that the team had nothing to wear for the game against the Cubs.

When Chicago owner Charles Murphy quit laughing over the Reds' predicament, he magnanimously offered to let them wear the Cubs' traveling jerseys, but Cincy declined. The thought of seeing every player in a Cubs' uniform was just too much to "bear."

Instead, Reds player-manager Joe Tinker telephoned across town and arranged with White Sox owner Charles Comiskey to borrow his team's road uniforms and some shoes for the day. Several Cincinnati players who refused to wear Sox footwear hustled off to the sporting goods store and bought new shoes. By game time, many uninformed fans were wondering why the Cubs were playing the White Sox in league play.

The Reds looked like orphans in ill-fitting hand-me-downs. Some of the jerseys were too big; others too small. A few sets of borrowed togs even affected the way Cincinnati played. Armando Marsans committed a rare miscue in center field and blamed it on his uniform—he was wearing the jersey of Sox shortstop Buck Weaver, who led the league in errors. While chasing a fly ball, right fielder Beals Becker ran right out of the oversized shoes he borrowed from Sox pitcher Big Ed Walsh! The Reds were so embarrassed they lost 7–2.

Eric McNair Oscar Melillo

Infielder **Infielder**
Boston, A.L. • **July 4, 1937**

Boston Red Sox infielders Eric McNair and Oscar Melillo hopped a train that took them straight to the state of embarrassment.

Following a tiring Fourth of July doubleheader at Fenway Park, the Red Sox and the Philadelphia Athletics were slated to leave Boston's South Station at midnight on separate trains. McNair and Melillo, both weary from the long day, couldn't wait to snuggle into their assigned berths on the sleeper.

As they were about to turn in, they noticed that their nearby bunkmates were a couple of A's. McNair and Melillo assumed the players had been traded to Boston and went over to welcome them. The A's players had perplexed looks on their faces because they thought the two Red Sox had been traded to Philly.

The truth was that McNair and Melillo had found their correct berth numbers—but on the wrong train!

By the time they discovered their error, the train had already left Beantown. Luckily, it had pulled out before the Red Sox sleeper had departed. Since both trains had to pass through Providence, Rhode Island, the two chagrined Boston players were able to get off in Providence and wait for their team's train to arrive. Melillo tried to drown out his embarrassment by playing his accordion loudly on the station platform until the Red Sox train pulled into town.

That wasn't the first time Melillo was confused over who his teammates were. On May 21, 1935, when Melillo was playing for the St. Louis Browns, he paid a social visit to the Red Sox clubhouse before a game between the two clubs. One of the Boston coaches came over and ordered him to take off his Browns uniform. Melillo thought it was because the Red Sox were concerned about fraternization. He was wrong.

"When you take off that uniform, put this one on," said the coach, handing the bewildered Melillo a Red Sox jersey. "You've just been traded to us for Moose Solters."

Bob Tillman

Catcher • **Boston, A.L.** • **August 5, 1962**

Like all catchers, Bob Tillman wore a mask, chest protector, shin guards, and glove. Unlike his colleagues, he could have used an extra piece of equipment—an alarm clock.

The Boston Red Sox catcher fell asleep at the most inopportune time during a game against the visiting Washington Senators at Fenway Park. In the fourth inning of a 2–2 tie, the Senators loaded the bases with Chuck Cottier at the plate. In such a crucial situation, the Bosox needed to stay on their toes. Tillman simply needed to stay awake.

Washington manager Sam Mele flashed the signal for the squeeze bunt. As Boston pitcher Hal Kolstad wound up, third base runner Ed Brinkman broke for the plate. The pitch was low and when Tillman caught it, he simply stayed on his haunches staring at the ground as if he were contemplating the binomial theorum. Meanwhile, Brinkman slid across the plate, stealing home without the dozing Tillman making any effort to tag him until it was far too late.

The sandman must have been in the ball park because Tillman wasn't the only player caught snoozing. Cottier, the batter, completely missed the squeeze sign and took the pitch. On the play, wide-awake runner Benny Daniels scampered from second to third for a double steal. It should have been a triple steal, but teammate Jimmy Piersall, who was on first, never made a move. He had joined Tillman in dreamland.

INSULTING INJURIES

No ball player wants to get hurt. But there are certain injuries that carry a subtle badge of honor—like getting spiked on a play at the plate or bruising a shoulder when crashing into the outfield fence. However, other injuries hurt the ego just as much as the body. For "The Most Ridiculous Injuries Ever Suffered," The Baseball Hall of SHAME inducts the following:

Goose Gossage   Cliff Johnson

Pitcher • New York, A.L.   Catcher • New York, A.L.
April 20, 1979

It was called The Bathroom Battle.

What started out as old-fashioned clubhouse needling blew up into a costly fistfight that sidelined New York Yankees relief ace Goose Gossage for ten weeks.

Even on a team that lives and breathes turmoil, the altercation between Goose and teammate Cliff Johnson stunned the Yankees. After all, the season was only twelve days old. Nevertheless, some good-natured barbs between a star and a benchwarmer stuck in each other's craws—and in their egos.

Gossage, who had signed a $2.7 million contract with New York, anchored the bullpen. The previous year he had led the league in saves with 27 and posted a sparkling 2.01 ERA. Johnson, on the other hand, was a part-time designated hitter and backup catcher with an anemic .184 batting average in 1978. Together, the two helped send the Yankee fortunes plunging.

After a loss to the Baltimore Orioles at Yankee Stadium, Gossage and Johnson were taking off their uniforms in front of their open lockers about thirty feet across from each other in the purple-carpeted Yankee clubhouse. While tossing barbs back and forth, Gossage threw a small rolled-up ball of tape at Johnson. When it sailed by him harmlessly, Cliff said, "I don't have to worry about you hitting me," a joke referring to a bad case of early-season pitching wildness that Goose was suffering.

From across the room, Reggie Jackson—who seems to have a nose for stirring up trouble—asked Johnson, "How'd you hit Goose when you were in the National League?" Before Cliff could answer, Goose piped up, "He swung at what he heard," meaning that Gossage had thrown his fastball by the big catcher. (And he had. During the 1977 season, Goose, then with the Pittsburgh Pirates, faced Johnson, then with the Houston Astros, three times and got him out on a grounder and two strikeouts.)

When the two players reached the showers, Johnson asked Gossage if he had meant what he said. "Yeah," the pitcher replied. Witnesses said Johnson then slapped Goose on the back of the head. Gossage thought the slap was too hard to be playful and he wheeled around and threw a punch at Johnson. The catcher retaliated by shoving Goose against the wall of the shower room. The players socked each other six or seven times before the coaches rushed in and pulled them apart.

After the fight, the gifted and expensive relief pitcher discovered that he had torn a ligament in the thumb of his pitching hand. He underwent surgery the very next day and was placed on the disabled list.

The Yankee brass was so upset that they fined both players ten days' pay—$18,603 for Gossage and $5,586 for Johnson. But the avoidable injury was even more costly for the team. The Yankees were in first place when The Bathroom Battle broke out. But without Gossage, the bullpen faltered badly. By the time Gossage returned to the bullpen on July 9, the Yankees were out of the pennant race. They finished in fourth place.

Freddie Fitzsimmons

Pitcher • New York, N.L. • March 26, 1927

During spring training in Miami, fat Freddie Fitzsimmons had survived the oppressive heat, the wind sprints, and the exercise workouts. But in 1927, there was one thing that got the better of the New York Giants' pitching star—his rocking chair.

One balmy evening after eating a big meal, Fitzsimmons settled into a rocking chair on the front porch of the club's hotel and chatted with teammates Rogers Hornsby and Bill Terry. During a lull in the conversation, Fitzsimmons dozed off. Terry and Hornsby chuckled at the sight of the snoring, rotund pitcher still rocking in his sleep.

Suddenly, Fitzsimmons awoke with a bloodcurdling yell. His companions thought he was reacting to a nightmare, but when they saw him grimace in pain and hold his pitching hand, they knew what had happened. While

Fitzsimmons was asleep, his right hand had slipped off his lap and got caught underneath the rocker. His fingers were flattened under the weight of his 190-pound body.

Although he didn't actually break any bones, Fitzsimmons was unable to get a proper grip on the baseball and missed several April starts for the Giants. It was a crucial injury because he had been the team's winningest pitcher the year before. Although he pitched well once he returned to the starting rotation, the Giants couldn't overcome his early-season absence. They finished third, only two games out.

"When he rocked on his hand, we laughed at him at first," recalled Terry. "But there weren't many of us laughing about it when the season was over."

Wade Boggs

Third Baseman • Boston, A.L. • June 9, 1986

"It's not the kind of injury you want to be known for, that's for sure," admitted a sheepish Wade Boggs.

He has fielded screaming line drives off his chest, barreled into second base to break up double plays, and taken errant fastballs on the hip without so much as uttering an "ouch." But getting undressed is another matter.

Boggs—touted as the only player today with the skill and coordination to possibly reach the coveted .400 mark in batting—showed a lamentable lack of skill and coordination off the field. He hurt himself seriously—while taking off his cowboy boots.

"I never expected something like this to happen," Boggs said. "I was in my hotel room in Toronto and I was pulling off my boots while standing up. The next thing I knew, I lost my balance and just fell over and banged my ribs against the arm of the couch. When I hit that couch, it hurt like hell. I couldn't breathe for five minutes and I thought I was dying."

Although Boggs didn't break any ribs, they were so sore that he missed a week of action. "It's hell to be uncoordinated," he joked. And then added, "Things are never dull with me around."

Once he returned to the lineup, Boggs sure took plenty of ribbing from his teammates over his embarrassing injury. No one would let him forget it—not even when he played in the All-Star Game a month later. As a gift for being selected for the team, the American League office gave Boggs and everyone else on the squad a pair of Justin cowboy boots.

Clarence "Climax" Blethen

Pitcher • Boston, A.L. • September 21, 1923

If ever there was a player who was caught in the teeth of a dilemma it was Climax Blethen.

Toward the end of the 1923 pennant race, with the Boston Red Sox bringing up the rear 37 games out of first, the club called up Blethen, a thirty-year-old rookie hurler, to gain a little major league experience.

Although he pitched like a rookie, he didn't look like one. Climax wore a set of false teeth that he stuck in his back pocket whenever he played. Without his choppers, Blethen appeared much older and more menacing on the mound than he really was.

Climax pitched briefly in relief in only five games, but his claim to shame came as a "pinched" runner.

In a game against the Detroit Tigers, Blethen was a runner on first when the next batter slapped a grounder to short. Climax went sliding into second to break up the double play. But he forgot that his false teeth were still in his back pocket.

When he slid into the base, his chompers clamped down on his butt. In every way imaginable, Climax was nipped at second.

Lefty Gomez

Pitcher • New York, A.L. • 1933

Lefty Gomez literally knocked himself right out of a game.

It was all because of his reputation as a lousy batter. Gomez, a Hall of Fame pitcher for the New York Yankees, collected more laughs than hits at the plate and wound up with a lifetime batting average of only .147.

Even Timmy Sullivan, the Yankees' batboy in Lefty's time, made fun of the hurler's batting incompetence. Once, as Gomez was heading for the on-deck circle, he said, "Get me my bat, Timmy." The batboy cracked back, "What are you planning to do with it?"

Then there was the memorable moment during the 1934 All-Star Game when Carl Hubbell struck out—in order—Babe Ruth, Lou Gehrig, Jimmy Foxx, Al Simmons, and Joe Cronin. Bill Dickey then broke the streak with a single, bringing Gomez up to the plate. Catcher Gabby Hartnett took one look at Lefty and razzed, "Are you trying to insult Hubbell, coming up here with a bat in your hands?" Gomez struck out.

Lefty was getting sick and tired of the jokes about his batsmanship. Finally, in a laugher of a game in which the Yankees held a 10-run lead, Gomez decided to work on his hitting.

"To get in the mood, I came to the plate with a bunch of bats on my shoulder—just like a slugger—and took a couple of hefty practice swings with the whole lot of them," he recalled. "I could hardly lift them, but I never let on. After careful deliberation, I selected one, looked at the center-field wall, and stepped to the plate.

"I leered at the pitcher, catcher, and umpire, which I am sure is part of the trick of hitting, and then started to knock the dirt out of my spikes with the end of the bat—like the big boys do."

Just then, teammate Frank Crosetti, who was waiting on deck, shouted, "Hey, Gomez." Lefty turned around and accidentally whacked himself right on the anklebone. He was in such pain that he had to be carried off the field and was laid up for several days.

Some of the players thought it was funny. But manager Joe McCarthy didn't. Said Gomez, "We were in the thick of a pennant fight at the time and McCarthy proceeded to tear my head off."

THE ONES WHO GOT AWAY

Unlike fishermen, baseball owners don't like to talk about the big ones that got away. Future sluggers and pitching stars have been hooked and then tossed away or allowed to wriggle free because some bait-brain in the front office couldn't recognize a prize catch if it jumped up and bit him. For "Teams That Foolishly Failed to Hold On to Future Superstars," The Baseball Hall of SHAME inducts the following:

Cardinals' Loss of Yogi Berra

1943

St. Louis Cardinals general manager Branch Rickey kept his eye on two Italian teenagers who played baseball in a poor section of town known as "The Hill." The boys were Joe Garagiola and Yogi Berra.

Rickey was impressed enough with Garagiola to give him a $500 signing bonus and shipped him off to the minors. Rickey thought Joe would become a star someday. Garagiola did—but as a sportscaster, not a ball player.

As for Berra, Rickey felt Yogi was too slow and awkward to invest any money in him. He told Berra, "You'll never be a ball player. Take my advice, son, and forget about baseball. Get into some other kind of business."

After being snubbed by the Cardinals, Yogi went to work pulling tacks at a shoe factory. He still played baseball for the fun of it, but his hopes of getting a professional contract seemed dim. However, a local official of the American Legion baseball program was convinced that Berra had great potential and contacted George Weiss, then the New York Yankees farm director. Based on glowing scouting reports, the Yankees signed Berra to a salary of $90 a month—and offered him the same $500 signing bonus that the Cardinals had given to Garagiola.

Just before leaving for his first minor league spring training camp in 1943, Yogi received a telegram from Rickey, who was now general manager of the Brooklyn Dodgers. Rickey had had a change of heart and asked Yogi to report to the Dodger camp where he would receive a contract and a bonus. But Rickey was too late.

Berra quickly worked his way through the minors and joined the Yankees in 1946. For the next seventeen years, he became one of the greatest, most popular catchers in baseball history. He was named MVP in the American League three times and was inducted into the Hall of Fame in 1972.

Red Sox Loss of Pee Wee Reese

1940

The last great shortstop the Boston Red Sox had was Hall of Famer Joe Cronin, the team's player-manager from 1935–45. They would have had another Hall of Fame shortstop as his successor if only Cronin hadn't been so shortsighted.

But Joe just couldn't see how a skinny little kid named Pee Wee Reese could ever replace him.

In 1938, the Boston Red Sox paid $195,000 for the Louisville Colonels minor league team for no other reason than to own the rights to Reese, Louisville's hottest prospect.

But Cronin was less than impressed when he saw Reese play for the first time in an exhibition game between the Red Sox and the Colonels. Pee Wee was a frail, pasty-faced kid who had suffered an illness during the off-season. "This is the guy who is going to take my job away from me?" Cronin asked incredulously.

Reese got off to a terrible start in Louisville in 1939 due to the aftereffects of his illness. Red Sox owner Tom Yawkey—influenced by Cronin's low opinion of Reese's playing ability—decided to sell Pee Wee. Hoping he could get at least $50,000 for him, Yawkey told Billy Evans, head of the farm system, to seek out the best offer. But there were no takers. "Not only isn't this guy a $50,000 ball player," Cronin said, "he isn't even a $5,000 ball player."

But in June, Reese began to hit and, more important, he began to field like a major league All-Star. The offers started coming in from other teams. Evans begged Cronin to come down to Louisville to take another look at Reese, but the manager refused. Yawkey, who took Cronin's word over Evans's, still wanted Reese sold. Brooklyn bought him for $150,000 and five players.

For the next sixteen years, Pee Wee anchored the infield for the Dodgers. His slick glove, clutch hitting, and leadership earned him respect, the team captaincy—and induction into the Hall of Fame in 1984.

Reese's success haunted Cronin. Time and again Joe felt compelled to deny reports that he had insisted the Red Sox sell Reese to protect his own job. "Honestly," Cronin admitted, "I didn't think the kid could make it."

Braves' Loss of Tom Seaver

1966

If it hadn't been for an absurd commissioner's ruling, Tom Seaver would have started his terrific major league career with the Atlanta Braves.

In 1966, the Braves drafted Seaver, a twenty-one-year-old pitching star for the University of Southern California, and signed him for a bonus of $50,000. Tom and his girlfriend Nancy were happy because the bonus money would give them the financial security they needed to set a wedding date. His parents were happy and planned a gala party for seventy of his closest friends. But one hour before the first cork was to pop, Braves general manager John McHale phoned Tom and gave him some shocking news: baseball commissioner William Eckert had voided the contract.

The problem was over the timing of the signing. The Braves had inked Seaver to a contract before USC's scheduled games began—but after the team had played two meaningless, spur-of-the-moment, preseason exhibition games with the Marines. Colonel Eckert, in all his militaristic wisdom, dropped the bomb that blew up the Braves' fortunes. He claimed that the Trojans' season had officially started when they played their unscheduled games with the Marines. Because it was against baseball rules for a major league team to sign a collegiate player once the season began, Eckert nixed Seaver's pact with the Braves.

Tom was disheartened but his party went on anyway. He figured he'd just rejoin the Trojans. But the NCAA declared him ineligible, even though he never received any payment from Atlanta. Suddenly, Seaver was not only $50,000 poorer, but he was also a man without a team, pro or college.

When it finally sank into the commissioner's head that both Tom and the Braves had signed in good faith, Eckert issued a new edict, giving Seaver a break while sticking it to Atlanta. The commissioner decreed that any club *except* the Braves that was willing to pick up the $50,000 bonus tab could put in a claim for Seaver. The Phillies, Indians, and Mets stepped forward, and as Tom listened via long-distance telephone, New York's name was picked out of a hat.

After only one year in the minors, Seaver took the National League by storm, winning 16 games for the Mets and recording a nifty ERA of 2.76 to cop Rookie of the Year honors in 1967. Seaver went on to win more than 300 games, mostly with the Mets and the Cincinnati Reds.

After watching Seaver repeatedly beat Atlanta, Braves president Bill Bartholomay ruefully thought about what might have been. "I feel sick every time I see Tom pitch," he moaned.

Dodgers' Loss of Roberto Clemente

1954

The Brooklyn Dodgers wanted to have their cake and eat it, too. Instead, they wound up with egg on their face.

The Dodgers were impressed with a twenty-year-old Puerto Rican prospect named Roberto Clemente and signed him to a bonus of $10,000. According to baseball law in 1954, a bonus baby had to be placed on the team's major league roster or be left unprotected in a minor league draft.

The Dodgers didn't want to carry an untested rookie on their roster because they were fighting for the pennant. But they didn't want to lose Roberto either.

So they assigned Clemente to their Triple-A farm team in Montreal and tried to "hide" him from all the other major league scouts by seldom playing him. That way, the Dodgers hoped, the scouts wouldn't notice Clemente and he wouldn't get picked by another team in the draft.

But the plan failed because of Clyde Sukeforth. After signing Clemente for Brooklyn, Sukeforth left the Dodgers and became a coach for the Pittsburgh Pirates. His new team sent him on a scouting mission to Montreal and Sukeforth saw enough to know that Clemente would blossom into a star. So the Pirates drafted the unprotected Roberto in 1954—and there was nothing the Dodgers could do about it. They had gambled and lost.

The Pirates were more than willing to find room on their major league roster for him in 1955. For the next eighteen years, Clemente electrified fans with his dazzling fielding, daring baserunning, and clutch hitting. The exciting outfielder batted over .300 in thirteen different seasons, led the Pirates to two World Championships, and was elected to the Hall of Fame.

Although the Dodgers' loss was the Pirates' gain, the reverse was also true. Pittsburgh had a chance to sign another future Hall of Famer, but ironically the team lost him to Brooklyn. The Pirates were impressed with a left-handed fastball pitcher from the University of Cincinnati by the name of Sandy Koufax. However, Pittsburgh offered him only $4,000 to sign. Koufax wanted more and the Dodgers were willing to give it to him. Making his debut in 1955—the same year as Clemente—Koufax developed over time into one of the game's greatest southpaws and strikeout artists. A three-time Cy Young Award winner, Koufax capped his remarkable career by being elected to the Hall of Fame in 1971.

THE BRAT PACK

The way some hotheaded players and managers behave, you'd swear there were two new teams in the majors—the Wet Hens and the Mad Hornets. When these guys are riled, they don't just fling bats, helmets, and towels out of the dugout. They breathe fire, foam at the mouth, and turn their wrath into a classic histrionic spectacle. For "The Wildest Temper Tantrums Ever Thrown," The Baseball Hall of SHAME inducts the following:

Lou Piniella

Outfielder • Kansas City–New York, A.L. • 1969–84
Manager • New York, A.L. • 1986–present

Lou Piniella didn't just wake up one morning with a terrible temper. He perfected it the way he perfected his hitting—while working his way up to the major leagues.

Sweet Lou showed flashes of an All-Star temper in the minors in 1967 when he was playing right field for the Portland Beavers of the Pacific Coast League. During one game, with his team trailing by a run, Piniella whiffed with the bases loaded to end the eighth inning. When he returned to the outfield, he was so aggravated that he kicked the fence with all his might. The fence fought back. As Lou walked away, a fifteen-foot section that he had booted toppled over on him, pinning him to the turf. The bullpen crew raced onto the field to lift the fence off him.

When the Kansas City Royals heard that Piniella could knock down fences, they had something else in mind and traded for him. As Rookie of the Year in 1969, Lou wielded a temper as hot as his bat. Once in a home game, Piniella grounded into a double play to end the contest. Naturally, he was upset. But rather than fling helmets and bats, Lou stormed all the way to the outfield gate, yanked it open, stalked out of the stadium, and hailed a cab home.

If he had continued to work out his anger that way, he would have saved the team money on plumbing bills. In his early days, Piniella's favorite way of venting his rage was smashing water coolers. One of the dugout coolers that he busted up at Kansas City Municipal Stadium is enshrined in the garage of his Tampa home. "I paid for it," he told a sportswriter, "so I might as well keep it."

When he was traded to the Yankees, Lou continued his angry assault on inanimate objects dumb enough to get in his way. Unfortunately, his rage also victimized innocent bystanders. One time he swatted a full cup of Gatorade and soaked trainer Gene Monahan. During another outburst, Piniella threw his batting helmet down so hard in disgust that it bounced off the dugout floor, striking manager Bob Lemon.

Rarely was Piniella's anger directed at people. Chickens, however, were another story. At the Kingdome in Seattle, Lou had the audacity to fling his glove at the famed and lovable San Diego Chicken. "Get him off the field!" Piniella barked at no one in particular as the winged wonder did his schtick between innings of a 3–1 Yankee loss. Still fuming after the game over the Chicken's antics, Lou declared that if he had had the chance, "I woulda kicked him in the butt."

Piniella occasionally sizzled over an official scorer's decision. In a game against Oakland in 1980, Lou hit what he thought was a double. When the scorer ruled it an error, thus taking a hit away from him, Piniella ranted at second base throughout the entire inning.

His hot temper failed to cool even when he finished playing and took over the managerial reins of the Yankees. Lou lasted all of 17 games before he unleashed his fury on an umpire and was ejected for the first time as manager. The heave-ho came for arguing over a third strike call and for bumping the ump.

Three months later, Piniella was in playing-day form, getting a deserved thumb for a dirt-kicking, hat-throwing exhibition. Afterward, he called home to wish his wife, Anita, a happy birthday. When she learned of his ejection, she sighed and said, "I'm forty-three and I'm still married to a four-year-old."

Johnny Allen

Pitcher • New York–Cleveland–St. Louis, A.L.
Brooklyn–New York, N.L. • 1932–44

Johnny Allen must've eaten sulfur and brimstone for breakfast. With a temper as explosive as Mt. St. Helens, Johnny blew his top and spewed his wrath upon umpires and teammates alike.

Afflicted with a chronic case of rage, the contentious hurler cursed umpires over every little call that went against him. Allen, thrown out of more games than scuffed-up baseballs, once worked himself into such a fury that he tried to bean an arbiter. Another time he actually assaulted one of the men in blue.

Johnny took aim on his own teammates as well. Whenever he lost a tough game, he blamed everyone but himself. Said teammate Lou Gehrig, "That guy thinks he should win every time he pitches, and that if he loses, it's a personal conspiracy against him."

After putting up with Allen's clubhouse tirades for four years, New York Yankees manager Joe McCarthy could no longer stand Johnny's constant ranting and blaming of others. McCarthy shipped the volcanic pitcher to the Cleveland Indians in the winter of 1935, whereupon a New York scribe told a Cleveland writer, "You have just acquired the worst disposition in the American League."

The change in scenery did little to temper Allen's temper. During one of his first games with the Indians, Johnny was accused by St. Louis Browns manager Rogers Hornsby of throwing spitballs. Hornsby ordered each of his players to have the umpire inspect the ball, but only after the catcher had tossed the ball back to Allen. The pitcher fumed over every such request until he finally exploded. When the next batter asked the ump to inspect the ball, Johnny didn't just lob the ball back. He drilled a fastball at the batter's head. The following inning, when the ump again called for the ball, Allen fired a bullet right at him. The startled arbiter saved himself from being hit by deflecting the speeding ball with his chest protector.

A few weeks later, after losing a tough 1–0 game in Boston, Johnny tried to douse the memory with a fire extinguisher at the Brunswick Hotel. First, he upended the stools in the hotel bar before taking the elevator to his floor. Then he overturned a large urn filled with sand and cigarette butts and scattered the contents all over the floor. Next, he grabbed a fire extinguisher off the wall and squirted it in all directions, including at a hapless maintenance man who was perched on a stepladder changing a light bulb. When Allen woke up the next morning, he was handed a bill from the hotel for $50 in damages and was fined $250 by the team.

Two years later, Johnny's temper generated even bigger headlines. Before pitching against the Boston Red Sox in Fenway Park, Allen cut the sleeve of

his sweatshirt so that his pitches would look like they were emerging from a tangled whirl of tattered strips.

In the second inning, after Bosox manager Joe Cronin complained, umpire Bill McGowan gave Allen an ultimatum: cut off the tattered sleeve, change shirts, or get thrown out of the game. Without a word, Johnny left the field. When he failed to return after five minutes, his manager, Ossie Vitt, went looking for him in the clubhouse. Vitt found Allen—in the showers. The stubborn and angry pitcher defied Vitt's order to return to the mound and was fined $250 on the spot.

The punishment didn't hurt Johnny one bit. In fact, he actually made money on the fine. The day after the incident, Allen's controversial shirt was on display in a show window of a downtown Cleveland store. "All Vitt did was make me pay $250," said Allen. "I sold the shirt to the store for $500."

In 1938, the angry pitcher showed a rookie what "down and dirty" meant in the bigs. Reporting to the Philadelphia Athletics fresh from the University of California campus, infielder Sam Chapman was immediately put into the lineup. It was just his luck that he had to face the fiery Allen in his first major league game.

"I was so nervous that Allen got two strikes on me before I stopped shaking," Chapman recalled. "I hit the next pitch and it struck him right below the kneecap. The shortstop got the ball and threw me out, but Allen was raging mad.

"He hollered at me, 'You busher! You'll never hit another ball like that!'

And I didn't either. I was on my back the rest of the day. Every time I came up, he'd whiz one past my ear."

After Johnny moved to the National League, he lost his mind during a game in Pittsburgh in 1943. Pitching for the Brooklyn Dodgers, Allen was charged with a balk by umpire George Barr. The hurler was so infuriated that he raced to the plate, grabbed Barr by the shoulders, and shook him until his cap fell off. Dodgers second baseman Billy Herman tried to intervene, but Allen pushed him aside. Then Brooklyn manager Leo Durocher ran out from the dugout and dropped Johnny with a tackle.

When Allen appeared to calm down, Durocher released his grip. But the red-hot pitcher blazed in anger again. So Leo tackled him a second time and teammate Les Webber applied a headlock which finally subdued him. Johnny drew a $200 fine and a thirty-day suspension.

Allen complained that all umpires were "fatheads" who were "trying to take away my living." However, after battling umpires for so many years, Johnny eventually decided that if you can't beat 'em, join 'em. In 1948, four years after retiring from baseball, Allen joined the ranks of his old enemies and became an umpire himself. He explained, "I just wanted to show them I could take it as well as I used to dish it out."

Dave Righetti

Pitcher • New York, A.L. • June 20, 1986

As an All-Star relief specialist for the New York Yankees, Dave Righetti saved a league-high 46 games in 1986. But he also suffered his most deplorable performance when he lost not only a big lead but his temper as well.

In the bottom of the ninth inning in a game against the Blue Jays in Toronto, Dave inherited an 8–2 lead from rookie Doug Drabek, who was only three outs away from his very first major league victory. Even though the Blue Jays had two runners on, it looked like an easy save for Righetti.

But he quickly found himself in hot water—and boiling mad. After letting in two runs and filling the bases, Dave served up a grand-slam homer to tie the game at 8–8.

Yankee manager Lou Piniella had seen more than enough. He started ambling toward the mound to summon reliever Brian Fisher while home plate umpire Don Denkinger tossed Righetti a new ball. Dave, who had suffered a miserable outing the night before, didn't want that ball or any other one. So he heaved it over the right-field wall more than 300 feet away. Piniella saved Denkinger the trouble of ejecting the sore loser by sending Dave to the showers.

Although New York went on to win the game in the 10th inning, virtually every Yankee steered clear of Righetti in the clubhouse. He showered and sat alone by his locker in solitude, and for the first time during the season, he refused to talk to the press.

"I don't think there's anything wrong with Righetti," Piniella told reporters after the game. "Actually, I was proud of him for the way he threw the ball over the wall." The former hothead smiled and added, "He reminded me of when I was playing."

Gene Mauch

Manager • Philadelphia–Montreal, N.L. • Minnesota–California, A.L. • 1960–present

When Gene Mauch explodes in anger, he throws more than just a temper tantrum—he throws food, bats, and anything else he can get his hands on.

His most celebrated food-flinging outburst came on September 22, 1963, in Houston. Mauch, then the manager of the Philadelphia Phillies, was burned to a crisp after his team lost 2–1 in the ninth inning on Joe Morgan's first big league hit.

Ungenial Mauch stalked into the clubhouse, where caterers Norm Gerdeman and his wife Evelyn had lovingly set out a beautiful post-game buffet of fresh fruit, cold cuts, salads, and their specialty, barbecued chicken and spareribs. For ten minutes, Gene paced up and down beside the food-laden table in the center of the room. Every time the incensed pilot walked by the buffet, he reached over, grabbed a handful of food, and threw it in one swift motion, as if attempting to cut down a runner at home. Salvos of watermelon and cantaloupe slices, potato salad, coleslaw, roast beef, and ham landed in the far corners of the room.

Then Mauch began chucking the ribs and chicken that the Gerdemans had prepared with such tender care. For a finale, he flipped over a pan of their special homemade barbecue sauce and sent it splashing into the open lockers of Wes Covington and Tony Gonzalez. Because the two players were unlucky enough to have their cubbyholes nearest the buffet table, their street clothes were ruined by food and sauce stains. When Gene cooled down, he apologized to both players and gave them $200 each to buy new suits.

In 1970, when Mauch was at the helm of the Montreal Expos, he again had a food fit in the visiting clubhouse in Houston after another gut-wrenching loss. Don Zimmer, then a coach with the Expos, recalled the scene:

"When we came into the clubhouse, there was a spread of eight big barrels of fried chicken. Now, when you lose a tough ball game, you need to go to your locker and sit there a few minutes and meditate before you go after the spread. That's what I did that night and I was starving.

"But Rusty Staub and another player went right to the table and filled

their plates as if the food was going out of style. Mauch was still steaming and he walked up behind them and said very sarcastically, 'Never mind us losing the game. Take care of your stomachs.'

"Then Mauch leaped up on the table and started spilling the chicken all over the place. He even put two of the tubs of chicken on the floor and jumped up and down on them. Wow! When he dumped the chicken, there were a couple of pieces left on the table. The minute he turned his back, I sneaked over and got those last two pieces of chicken. That's how hungry I was."

When Gene wasn't tossing food, he was heaving bats onto the field. During a game against the Boston Red Sox on July 16, 1978, Mauch, then the manager of the Minnesota Twins, thought first base umpire Bill Kunkel was blind as a bat—so he threw some to underscore his point.

Gene, who had been thumbed out of the game after arguing with Kunkel, grabbed the Twins' bats by the handful in the dugout and sent them sailing onto the field. He littered the diamond with dozens of pieces of lumber before huffing off to the clubhouse. Afterward, Mauch explained to reporters, "I was taking my bats home and they just slipped out of my hands."

Sometimes, instead of throwing things in anger, he kicked them. His most famous boot came on May 7, 1969, in Atlanta during a game between the Braves and the Expos. Gene became enraged after a balk had been called against his pitcher, Mike Wegener, allowing the tying run to score. After losing the debate with the umpires, Mauch charged to the mound, kicked the resin bag ten feet in the air, ran after it, and booted it another twenty feet. Then he grabbed the ball from Wegener and punted it high into the sky. Gene was thrown out before the ball ever touched the ground.

Roaring mad after losses, Mauch has ripped clubhouse phones off walls, thrown bats through windows, and busted doors and furniture. Otherwise, he's one of the nicest guys in baseball. Gene has always been a manager with a split personality. For example, after his Phillies dropped a 4–3 decision to the Cincinnati Reds on May 12, 1965, Mauch locked reporters out of the clubhouse, broke a window, and jammed his fist into a dressing-room locker. However, the next night, after the Phils knocked off the Reds 7–6, Gene was all smiles. He greeted the sportswriters at the clubhouse door and innocently asked them, "Where were you guys last night?"

Hi Bithorn

Pitcher • Chicago, N.L. • July 15, 1942

Chicago Cubs pitcher Hi Bithorn threw more than just a conniption fit when he was taunted by his opponents.

Unable to ignore the incessant bench jockeying of Brooklyn Dodgers manager Leo Durocher, Bithorn blew up on the mound and tried to silence his tormentor by firing a beanball at him—while Leo was still in the dugout.

Durocher, cold-blooded enough to make antifreeze commercials, had deliberately tried to provoke Bithorn. It was part of a devious scheme that Leo had concocted before his Dodgers faced the Cubs at Wrigley Field. "Let's get their goat," he told his players. "Let's heckle the hell out of them."

Other than for the sport of it, there was little need to harass the lowly Cubs. They had lost eight of their previous ten meetings with the first-place Dodgers and trailed Brooklyn by 18½ games, so far back they couldn't even dream about the pennant race.

Nevertheless, the Dodgers launched an all-out attack with their mouths. Heading into the fifth inning trailing 5–2, the Cubs managed to ignore the teasing—except for their relief pitcher, Hi Bithorn. His hair bristled and his teeth gnashed as the Dodger bench, led by master motor mouth Durocher, rode him unmercifully.

The more Bithorn saw red, the less he saw the plate. He walked the first two batters in the fifth, which naturally spurred the bench jockeys to even greater verbal badgering. Bithorn became more provoked and heaved a wild pitch over the catcher's head and back to the screen. Welling with anger, the seething pitcher walked another batter and, following a fielder's choice, gave up a run-scoring single. Unable to keep his mind on the game, Bithorn issued his fourth free pass of the inning, loading the bases and raising the volume of the Dodgers' heckling.

Chicago manager Jim Wilson realized that Bithorn was in no shape to pitch anymore and called in another reliever. But before Wilson had a chance to get the ball from Bithorn, the sizzling-mad pitcher stormed toward the Brooklyn dugout and hurled a beanball at Durocher. But Bithorn failed to nail him or any other Dodger.

"Hey, amigo," Durocher shouted to the Puerto Rican–born pitcher. "You didn't have any control on the mound, so no wonder you couldn't hit any of us."

George Brett

Third Baseman • Kansas City, A.L. • 1973–present

George Brett has proven that he's one of baseball's best hitters—of paint cans, garbage pails, and urinals.

With a temper as quick as his stroke, the Kansas City star has wreaked havoc on more than just an opposing pitcher's ERA. Whenever he's in a rare slump and having trouble whacking baseballs, he takes out his frustration by whacking anything in his path.

Brett was wanted in Baltimore for assault and battery on several large cans of beige paint. During a game on May 9, 1986, against the Orioles at Memorial Stadium, George flew into a rage after striking out. Clenching his bat in a death grip, he stormed into the runway leading from the visitors' dugout to the clubhouse. There, he spotted the paint cans which had been left by city workers for a job they were planning to do the next day. Brett took it upon himself to do the paint job for them. Unlike the pitches he couldn't hit during the game, George connected with every vicious swing of his bat on the cans. In fact, he belted those cans so hard that he broke his bat and went back for another one. By the time his outburst subsided, Brett had splintered three bats and splattered beige paint on the floor and walls of the runway. The scene looked like a bad imitation of a Jackson Pollock painting.

In 1980, George won the Most Valuable Player award. The following year, he had another MVP season—for Most Vexed Player. Mired in a batting slump, he was never more ornery. "I've been screaming in the outfield during batting practice," he admitted to the press at the time. "I even started yelling at the bugs attacking me." After injuring his ankle in a game on May 14, 1981, he whomped a photographer on the head with a crutch. Brett, who apologized the next day, later found a pair of new crutches in his locker. One had his name on it. The other had a sign that read, "For Photographers Only."

Two weeks later, on May 29, an exasperated Brett went three rounds with the rest room behind the dugout at Metropolitan Stadium in Minneapolis. The rest room lost. After feebly grounding out with runners on base, the All-Star third baseman charged into the rest room with his bat and clubbed two toilets and a sink into little pieces. The Royals apologized to the Twins for George's batting exhibition and enclosed a check for $1,400 to cover the damage costs.

At year's end, *TV Guide* hung Brett with runner-up honors in its annual listing of bad-boy images. (George Steinbrenner won, after his celebrated fistfight with a fan in an elevator at the World Series.) Maybe it was coincidence, but Lifebuoy soap, 7-Up, and Redman tobacco dropped Brett from further commercial endorsements.

Although George's temper tantrums aren't as wild as they used to be, he still can throw a nasty fit.

"The people around Royals Stadium know better than to get in Brett's way when he has one of those days," said a sportswriter who covers the team. "Someone came up with the clever idea of putting a big plastic garbage pail down in the runway leading to the dugout. George goes after it with his bat when he strikes out a lot or is in a slump. It's known as George's can. It's a really tough one that's supposed to be almost indestructible. But it's all beat to hell."

BOOING THE BOO BIRDS

Fans come to the ball park to watch a game and engage in one of America's favorite pastimes—booing. At the umpire, the gopher ball pitcher, the slumping slugger. However, sometimes the real boos shouldn't be directed at the playing field, but right up to the stands, where fans have displayed some of the rudest, raunchiest, rowdiest behavior this side of a riot zone. For "The Most Unruly Behavior of Fans," The Baseball Hall of SHAME inducts the following:

Pete "Leather Lung" Adelis

Philadelphia A's Fan • 1940–55

Pete Adelis—better known as "The Leather Lung of Shibe Park"—was baseball's most loathsome heckler.

More obnoxious than Howard Cosell and more insulting than Don Rickles, Adelis stood six feet tall, weighed 260 pounds, wore a size-52 coat—and owned a booming voice to match.

He was such a tenacious tormentor that his favorite team, the hometown Philadelphia Athletics, once took him on the road to harangue their opponents. The New York Yankees, among his most abused targets, tried to get on his good side by giving him free tickets to Yankee Stadium. It worked. More than once they imported him to New York to intimidate their foes (but never the A's).

Like a gumshoe who enjoys digging up dirt, Adelis, who died in 1982, diligently collected juicy tidbits on the private lives of the players and then bellowed out the malicious gossip for all the players and fans to hear. "When Pete boomed out something personal, you could see the player just start shaking," recalled his brother Walter.

"Pete used little known facts like if a player was out the night before with some woman and got drunk. These were things a player just wouldn't expect to hear on the field. The player would say to himself, 'Who is this guy and how did he know about that?' The things he yelled at them really surprised and shamed them. They just couldn't escape his voice because it carried all over the park."

More than one player wished Leather Lung would have been barred from ever entering a ball park. "One of the players Pete got on the most was Pat Seerey, an outfielder for the Chicago White Sox in 1948," recalled Walter Adelis. "It so happened that Pete and I were in New York to see the Yankees on the day Seerey hit four home runs against the A's at Shibe Park. After the game, Seerey wanted to know where Pete was. Seerey figured that the only reason he had such a good day was because Pete wasn't there."

Flag-hating Radicals

Dodger Stadium • April 25, 1976

Two misguided protestors had the audacity to try to set the American flag on fire during the middle of a baseball game. They struck out.

In the bottom of the fourth inning in a game against the visiting Chicago Cubs, the Los Angeles Dodgers were at bat when two spectators ran onto the playing field near Cub outfielders José Cardenal and Rick Monday. "I saw the clowns come on the field, and I thought they were out there just to prance around," Monday recalled. "But then they began spreading out the American flag as if it was a picnic blanket."

Monday's first instinct was to "just run them over," he said. But when he noticed they were fumbling around with a lighter and a can of fluid, he swooped in—like Paul Revere at full gallop—and snatched the flag. Fans cheered wildly as Monday carried Old Glory out of danger and handed it to a member of park security. Meanwhile, one of the foiled radicals threw the can of lighter fluid at Monday in disgust and fled from the field.

Reflecting on his flag-rescue mission, Monday said, "If you're going to burn the flag, don't do it in front of me. I've been to too many veterans' hospitals and seen too many broken bodies of guys who tried to protect it."

When the veteran center fielder went to bat in the next inning following the attempted flag desecration, he drew a standing ovation from the fans while the mammoth left-field message board flashed: "Rick Monday . . . You made a great play!"

Gate Crashers

Ebbets Field • September 7, 1924

Denied admission to Ebbets Field because the game was sold out, about 8,000 irate fans tore the heavy entrance gates off their hinges and stormed into the park like battle-mad troops.

It was the wildest—and most deplorable—day in the checkered history of the famed Brooklyn ball yard.

Hours before the home team was slated to play the crosstown arch rival New York Giants for sole possession of first place, fans streamed into Ebbets Field. The demand for tickets was so great that club officials decided to let spectators stand in foul territory. When this unusual provision failed to accommodate the entire crowd, officials slammed the gates, shutting out thousands of peeved fans, including hundreds of late-arriving ticket holders.

The angry mob was not to be denied. Overpowering the woefully small contingent of policemen, the determined fans split into two flanks. One group, armed with crowbars and poles, battered down the main gate and crashed through the turnstiles while thousands of other nonpaying spectators climbed up and over the walls of the outfield.

Almost every square inch of foul territory and the deepest part of the outfield were occupied by fans. As the game wore on, the crowd continually encroached on the playing field. At times Giants manager John McGraw was unable to see all his players on the field, so he ordered his coaches to stand on top of the dugout where they informed him of his players' whereabouts.

Throughout the game, Brooklyn fans showered the Giants with enough white confetti to make the field look as though it had been covered with a light snow. Making things even tougher for the teams, the rabble-rousers tossed their straw hats onto the infield whenever Brooklyn scored a run.

Conditions became intolerable in the bottom of the ninth inning with New York ahead 8–4. When Eddie Brown lifted a fly ball to center field, Hack Wilson was completely enveloped by the spectators and couldn't make the otherwise easy catch. Giants captain Frankie Frisch ordered the game stopped until the umpires and police could clear the playing field. Without the help of the crowd, a valiant Brooklyn rally fell short and New York held on for an 8–7 victory.

The Who Fans

Thanks to thousands of rock-concert fans, Anaheim Stadium went to pot. Marijuana, that is.

Just days before the California Angels were ready to play their 1976 home opener at the park, groundskeepers discovered about 500 marijuana plants growing wild in the outfield. The pot sprouted shortly after the rock group The Who held a concert there that drew 55,000 fans, including about 10,000 who were allowed to sit in the outfield.

The most destructive fans were those who couldn't obtain tickets to the concert. They became abusive and pushed against the center-field wall until about seventy feet of the fence was knocked down. Workers managed to repair the fence with just a few hours to spare before the Angels' opener.

Apparently, the rock fans who sat on the field left "tokin" reminders of their attendance. Days later, the wrong kind of grass began growing along the left-field foul line and in a large patch in center field. The baby marijuana plants had flourished when the grounds crew watered and fertilized the outfield grass (the regular kind).

Anaheim city officials decided it was high time to wipe out the marijuana with a herbicide. Stadium manager Tom Liegler then told head groundskeeper Joe Verdi to turn down any volunteers who wanted to help rid the field of the illegal weed—even if they were willing to work for nothing.

Dave Parker Tormentors

At age twenty-nine, Pittsburgh Pirates slugger Dave Parker seemed to have everything. Money, talent, Gold Gloves, batting titles—and fans who wanted to maim him.

That's because a group of moronic hometown fans made Parker the target of loud boos and thrown objects. During the home opener, an idiot hurled a tightly wrapped bag of nuts and bolts at Dave's head. A bat was tossed at him from the stands on Bat Day. After months of torment, the star outfielder was finally forced to flee the field, fearing for his life.

On July 20, 1980, a day when Pirates captain Willie Stargell was honored, Parker was humiliated—and scared. He was playing right field in the eighth inning of the first game of a doubleheader against the visiting Los Angeles Dodgers. Suddenly, a jerk in the stands hurled a nine-volt, two-inch radio battery at Dave's head. It whizzed by his left ear like a Nolan Ryan fastball. When the battery hit the turf, it bounced 200 feet toward first base. "I could hear it go by me," Parker said. "It was too close for comfort. I wasn't going to stand there and give him another shot." So Dave—who is so tough he once returned to the lineup just fifteen days after breaking his jaw—called time and left the playing field. He didn't return for the rest of the day, sitting out the second game, too.

"I did it because this is my life, my livelihood," he said. "I just can't risk getting hurt."

Pirates vice president Harding Peterson was so appalled over the assault with battery that he announced to the fans before the start of the second game: "Should there be a next time for this needless and childish activity, there is a strong possibility that the entire Pirate team will be removed from the field, even at the expense of forfeiting the game. The Pirate management is sick and tired of these acts, admittedly performed by a handful of our spectators."

Parker's relationship with Pittsburgh fans deteriorated because of six million reasons—the dollars of his contract. His detractors claimed he wasn't worth what he was paid. At the time of the battery incident, slightly more than halfway through the 1980 season, Dave had a .286 batting average, 12 homers, and 53 RBIs. He was also the top vote-getter for the All-Star Game. But for many overly demanding and ignorant fans that still wasn't good enough.

After the doubleheader, Reggie Smith of the Dodgers—himself a target of a thrown object at Yankee Stadium during the 1977 World Series—told Parker, "Fans don't throw things at mediocre or poor players. I guess you have to be good to be hated."

Mickey Mantle Fans

Yankee Stadium • May 30, 1980

Mickey Mantle was mugged. In Yankee Stadium. By his own fans!

Right in his own backyard, the beloved star was accosted, robbed, punched, and mauled. So serious was the disgraceful assault that Mantle was rushed to the hospital for treatment of a bruised jaw.

The attack happened after Mickey caught a fly ball for the final out in a Memorial Day doubleheader. Before he could reach the safety of the dug-out, he was engulfed in a sea of swarming fans who spilled onto the playing field.

Mantle quickly realized that these were not just shiny-eyed tykes who were worshiping their hero from a respectful distance. These were obnoxious members of an ugly, unruly mob who were dead set on snaring a souvenir of the Mick.

They closed in on Mantle like hungry lions on a fallen gazelle. The fans

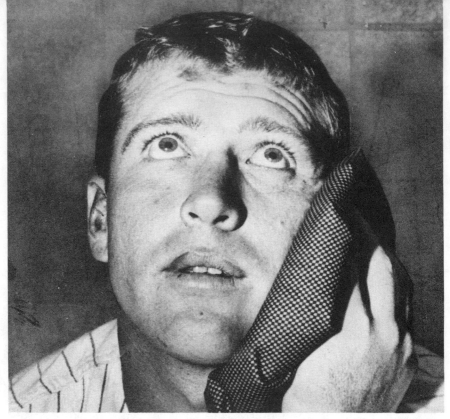

tried—and succeeded—in stealing his cap. Then they tried to swipe his glove. They clawed at his jersey, and when he resisted, they pummeled him. Someone slugged him in the jaw. In desperation, Mantle lowered his head and barreled his way through the crowd to the dugout. He was then taken to the hospital for X rays and treatment and placed on a soft-food and liquid diet.

"They grabbed my cap and nearly put out my eye in the process," said Mickey, holding an ice pack to his injured and swollen jaw. "They were grabbing and clawing at my glove. I finally put my head down and bulled through the pack like a fullback.

"You have to protect yourself in a situation like that. I warded off people with my hands, but it was more like swimming the breaststroke than punching or even straight-arming. I guarantee I got more bruises out of it than anyone, though I do remember someone going down when he banged into my shoulder. Incidentally, he was no kid. He was at least as big and as old as I am."

And all this happened to a player whom the fans *adored*!

They really got vicious when Mantle declined to sign autographs after home games. Whenever he came through the clubhouse door, he scrambled through a gauntlet of hundreds of wild-eyed kids. Afraid of getting hurt by the frenzied mob, Mickey ignored their pleas for autographs. This only infuriated the scorned young fans, who then cursed, grabbed, spit, jabbed pencils, and squirted ink at him.

Mantle hated the ink-flippers the most. Holding their fountain pens low so they couldn't be seen, odious punks snapped their pens at Mickey as he passed, sending streaks of blue ink splattering down the leg of his pants.

"The same kids are there every day," Mantle complained to the press. "I'd never give any of them an autograph now because I might be giving it to one of the little so-and-sos who flipped ink on me."

Playoff Lovers

Polo Grounds • October 3, 1951

When Bobby Thomson hit his dramatic "shot heard 'round the world" in the 1951 playoffs, every Giants rooter in the Polo Grounds was losing his head, except for one unabashed female fan who was giving it.

Thomson and the two teammates he drove in weren't the only ones who scored on his historic pennant-winning homer. Amid tens of thousands of deliriously happy fans swarming onto the field in the sport's wildest climax, one guy was enjoying one of a different kind.

For everyone else in the ball park, sex was the farthest thing from their minds. It was the bottom of the ninth inning of the third and final National League playoff game, and the Brooklyn Dodgers were winning 4–2. The Giants were threatening with runners on second and third, one out, and slugger Bobby Thomson at the plate. "You could cut the tension in that ball park with a knife," recalled spectator Arnold Winick in a published interview. "Everyone was nervous, and it wasn't just ordinary nervousness. It was the kind that ate your stomach up, that rang in your head like a Chinese gong without let-up."

Then Thomson smacked the most-talked-about home run in baseball, launching the Giants into the World Series and sending fans into orbit. "The next thing I knew, I was down on the field, trying to get at one of the players just to touch him," Winick recounted. "You've never seen such an outpouring of pure hysterical glee. It was like a million people all having a communal orgasm."

At least one fan *was* having one, thanks to a willing, shameless young woman. Said Winick, "I saw a man and a woman lying in the dirt along the railing by the first-base boxes, right next to the dugout, and he had his fly open and she was . . . you know. There was a big crowd around them, but nobody was paying a bit of attention to them."

Some were. Robert O'Brien, in the same published interview, said, "I saw the same thing. I saw newspaper photographers taking pictures of the two people, but of course they never got published."

Winick had an idea why the lovers engaged in a sex act in the midst of one of the great moments in baseball history: "I think she was paying off a bet."

Confetti-bombing Cubs Fan

Wrigley Field • June 9, 1963

A jerk in the right-field bleachers at Wrigley Field ignited a firestorm of needless trouble when he bombarded an outfielder with confetti in the middle of a play.

While spectators were enjoying an action-packed slugfest between the visiting Los Angeles Dodgers and the Chicago Cubs, one devious Cubs fan was plotting a surprise attack by busily tearing up scorecards and newspapers. He had been waiting and hoping for just the right moment to blitz enemy outfielder Frank "Hondo" Howard. The schemer reasoned that since Howard looked confused on fly balls hit to him even under the best of circumstances, imagine how befuddled he would be trying to catch one descending from a shower of shredded paper.

Zero hour came in the bottom of the sixth inning with the Dodgers ahead 8–6. After Cubs catcher Dick Bertell singled, pinch hitter Bob Will lofted a drive to deep right field where Howard drifted back to the ivy-covered wall. Just as Hondo was about to make the catch, the bomber in the front row of the bleachers let loose a cannonade of confetti that rained upon the hapless outfielder. The sneak attack then triggered an explosion of confusion and outrage.

Flustered by the salvo of shredded paper, Howard failed to make the catch. The ball glanced off his glove and fell among the confetti that had collected on the warning track.

Although the bombardment was meant to help the Cubs, it befuddled them, too. Bertell held up between first and second because he thought Howard had caught the fly. The runner couldn't see the ball through all the shredded paper. But by then, Will had run right into Bertell and, for a brief moment, had actually passed him before turning back to first for a single. Fortunately for the Cubs, the umpires didn't notice the infraction.

However, while all eyes were on the play in right, Dodger benchwarmer Lee Walls saw from his team's first base dugout that Will had passed Bertell on the base path. When Walls argued the case a little too vigorously with the umps, he was thrown out of the game.

Meanwhile, Dodgers manager Walter Alston launched a major beef, arguing that the fan had interfered with Howard. But the arbiters ruled that he couldn't have caught it anyway and walked away. (Hondo stayed in the majors because of his bat, not his glove.) The Dodgers survived the paper raid and went on to win 11–8. The bleacherite may have successfully dropped a bomb, but in the eyes of players and other fans, he laid an egg.

Baseball's MBAs

Those who can, do. Those who can't, teach. Those who can't do either, manage. And sometimes they don't do that very well. In fact, they'd have trouble managing a Little League team. The lucky ones can mishandle the players, screw up the lineup, make the wrong moves, and still win because the team has talent. But if they have no gifted players to hide behind, their mismanagement becomes glaring enough for all to see. For "Dishonorary Degrees for Managers of Blundering Actions," The Baseball Hall of SHAME inducts the following:

Wilbert Robinson

Manager • Brooklyn, N.L. • 1914–31

Wilbert Robinson didn't manage a baseball team. He directed an on-going comedy. And he starred as the clown.

Although beloved by the Brooklyn fans, Uncle Robbie mismanaged the Dodgers to dizzying lows. In his eighteen years as the Brooklyn pilot, he misled his team to a second-division finish twelve times. When it came to strategy, he threw the book away; in fact, he never even read it.

He managed by gut, of which the 300-pound skipper had plenty. As the father of the Daffiness Boys, Robinson tossed aside conventional wisdom like a broken bat. Sometimes he let waiters at his favorite restaurant pick his starting pitchers. Other times he asked baseball writers to choose his lineup. And he even took managerial advice from his wife, Ma Robinson.

Once, at her suggestion, he started a rookie pitcher against the Chicago Cubs. The kid was mauled for 12 runs before Robinson went out to the mound and gave him the hook. As Uncle Robbie headed back to the dugout, he walked by Ma Robinson's box seat and snapped, "I hope you're satisfied. I started the kid like you suggested. Now maybe you'll do less second-guessing."

Robinson's mind worked in mysterious ways; that is, when it worked. One day in 1927, he decided to start fringe player Oscar Roettger in the outfield. But when Robinson was writing out the lineup card, he didn't know how to spell Roettger's name. "What the hell," muttered the flustered manager, "maybe I should start Gus Felix." He did, too.

That wasn't the first time the lineup card gave Robinson trouble. Before one game, he handed the home plate umpire what he thought was the lineup. It turned out to be Uncle Robbie's laundry list.

The rotund manager often showed too much compassion for his team's own good. For example, in 1927 the Dodgers were in the midst of a rousing rally when benchwarmer Chick Fewster began pounding a bat on the dugout steps and whooping it up. "Cut that out," Robinson ordered. Pointing to the far end of the bench where pitcher Jesse Petty was fast asleep, Robbie said, "I don't want you to wake up old Jesse."

For all his hilarious faults as a manager, none were more glaring than his screw-ups while coaching at third base. One of his most embarrassing moments came during a game in 1923 after Dodgers catcher Zack Taylor blasted a late-inning extra-base hit. As Taylor chugged into third base, Robinson grabbed him and gave him a big congratulatory bear hug. But it was short-lived. Uncle Robbie's hug pulled Taylor off the bag and the player was tagged out by the third baseman.

Robinson never quite got the hang of coaching signs—a rather critical problem for a manager. A classic case in point came in the ninth inning of a tight game in 1924 when Brooklyn slugger Zack Wheat stepped to the plate. It was a situation that demanded a sacrifice. Wheat knocked the dirt from his spikes and stared at Robinson coaching at third. Uncle Robbie didn't flash a sign. Perplexed, Wheat backed away from the plate and looked again. Still no signal.

Poor Uncle Robbie had forgotten the bunt sign! He ran his fingers uncertainly across the lettering on his uniform. He tugged at his earlobe. He scratched his arm. Nope, those weren't right. Finally, in desperation, he went into a crouch and extended his hands in the unmistakable gesture of a man dropping a bunt.

Now everyone in Ebbets Field knew that Wheat had been ordered to bunt. Trying to thwart the sacrifice attempt, the pitcher fired a high inside pitch. But rather than bunt, Wheat walloped the ball over the fence into Bedford Avenue. When Wheat rounded third, Robinson gave him an affectionate slap on the seat of his pants. The manager had already forgotten that Wheat had ignored his orders.

Signals confused not only Robinson but his players as well. During a team meeting one day, outfielder Babe Herman spoke up. "Let's cut out signs, Robbie. We don't get 'em anyway." Robinson agreed and the Daffiness Boys played without signs for a week. Naturally, chaos reigned at the plate and on the base paths. So Robinson called another team meeting. "Our trouble ain't signs," he announced. "It's having too many dumbbells who think they're smart managers. From now on, I'm the only dumbbell giving signals around here."

Walter "Rabbit" Maranville

Manager • Chicago, N.L. • July 7–September 3, 1925

To the irrepressible, fun-loving Rabbit Maranville, life was a joke. So was his brief stint as manager.

The Rabbit—so named because of his large ears and small 5-foot, 5-inch, 145-pound body—was an incredibly gifted shortstop but an incredibly lousy manager. As a player, he lasted twenty-three years in the majors. As a manager, he lasted only eight weeks. The big surprise was that he even survived that long.

In the summer of 1925, the Chicago Cubs fired manager Bill Killefer and unwisely appointed their impish thirty-three-year-old shortstop to the job. That was like making Dennis the Menace a high school principal.

Obviously, the Chicago brass had faulty memories. They forgot about his bouts with John Barleycorn and his penchant for perilously walking on hotel ledges. They forgot about the times he faked his own murder and his own suicide just for laughs. Instead they hired a man who once speared a live goldfish in a restaurant fountain and ate it, who once fell off an auditorium stage and broke his leg in an impromptu sliding demonstration; who once arranged to have a teammate chase him through Times Square hollering "Stop, thief!"

The Cubs had hired a vaudevillian, not a manager. In his first move as skipper, the Rabbit prowled through a Pullman car at night and poured ice water on every player he caught sleeping. "No sleeping under Maranville management, especially at night," he ordered.

Soon after his appointment, Maranville arrived with his team in New York, where he triggered a wild street brawl. The manager and two of his players had gotten into a cab outside the Hotel Astor. A short time later, they concluded that the cabby was trying to cheat them by going around the same block twice. Indignantly, they ordered the driver to let them out. When they failed to tip him, the driver called them cheapskates, whereupon the trio gave him a generous helping of fists. It took a squad of policemen to break up the fight. After the three Cubs and the driver spent the night in jail, they loyally refused to testify against each other and were released.

Chicago management was not amused by the Rabbit's escapades. In fairness to Maranville, he did follow through on his promise to lead the team out of seventh place. He led the Cubs into the cellar. Under his stewardship, Chicago won 23 and lost 30.

By September, Maranville knew his days as field general were numbered. So in a final act of one-upmanship, he scooped the press on his own firing. Pretending to hawk newspapers outside Ebbets Field before a game, the Rabbit shouted, "Extra! Extra! Read all about it! Maranville fired!" And so he was. The very next day.

Billy Martin

Manager • New York, A.L. • September 20, 1985

Billy Martin was just itching to get into trouble—and literally rubbed the Yankees the wrong way.

The volatile skipper scratched his nose at the worst possible moment and helped trigger a rally that defeated his team during a tight pennant race.

Martin put his nose out of joint in a rare mental lapse when he didn't pay attention to one of his own signs—the one for a pitchout. His signal for a pitchout was rubbing his schnozz.

In the bottom of the seventh inning of a 2–2 game against the Baltimore Orioles, the O's had two outs with runner Alan Wiggins on first and Lee Lacy at the plate. Before the first pitch to Lacy, Yankees catcher Butch Wynegar glanced over to the New York dugout. It just so happened at that exact moment Martin had an itchy nose and rubbed it. Naturally, Wynegar assumed his manager had ordered a pitchout. So the catcher called for one, and pitcher Rich Bordi complied, much to Martin's surprise. Wiggins wasn't running and Lacy drew ball one.

After the count went to 2–and–0, Wynegar saw Martin scratch his proboscis again. Surely Martin had stolen the Orioles' signs, thought Wynegar, who ordered another pitchout which Bordi threw for ball three. Now way behind in the count, Bordi eventually walked Lacy. The next two batters drove in run-scoring singles and the Yankees went on to lose 4–2. It was New York's eighth straight loss and all but squelched their last-ditch drive to catch the eventual division winners, the Toronto Blue Jays.

After the game, Martin, who had seen just about everything else go wrong in the past week, admitted he should have known better. "At first, I couldn't believe it when I saw the pitchout. I couldn't understand why Butch called for it. Then," Martin said with his voice lowering, "I realized what *I* had done."

Tommy Lasorda

Manager • Los Angeles, N.L. • 1978

Tommy Lasorda not only led his Los Angeles Dodgers to the World Series in 1978, he also led them to distraction.

"If there was anything that got Tommy more tense than losing, it was winning," said former Dodger hurler Burt Hooton. "I think fighting it out for first place all year got to him."

Following almost every game, Lasorda couldn't wait to gab with the press. But after a bitter defeat in San Diego on May 23, 1978, he stepped completely out of character and shut his open-door policy with mortifying consequences. Irate over five Dodger errors that triggered a 3–2 loss, Lasorda lost his cool. In the clubhouse, Tommy angrily knocked over chairs, tables, and clothes bins.

Then he charged into his office and slammed the door so hard that the lock broke. When he cooled down and tried to open the door, Lasorda found he was locked in. He started yelling and banging on the door.

"I think a lot of the guys who were covering the Dodgers felt it was poetic justice," said one of the team's beat writers. "He slammed the door to keep us out, and then when he discovered he couldn't get out, he went into a rage. We loved it. Tommy was in there screaming his head off and nobody would help him at first." Finally one of the players found a maintenance man who freed Lasorda.

"In the year we won the pennant, it seemed that if you blinked your eye wrong, Tommy fined you," said Hooton. "It was done in fun, but he sure came up with some strange stuff."

His strangest was the car pool incident. Occasionally Lasorda car-pooled to home games with Hooton and Dodger players Tommy John, Charlie Hough, and Bill Russell because they all lived in the same area.

One Sunday, when it was Lasorda's turn to pick up the others, he dawdled here and dawdled there. At the John home, Lasorda spent twenty minutes playing with the children and then he chatted amiably with the players' families at the other stops. Next, Tommy pulled into a donut shop and bought some goodies after waiting in a long, slow line. By the time the five Dodgers arrived at the ball park, it was thirty minutes past the deadline for players to be in uniform.

"I'm fining each of you $50 for being late," Lasorda told his carpool mates.

"But, Tommy, we were with you," Hooton protested.

"That should teach you," the manager replied, "that when you have to be somewhere at a certain time, you should go with someone who is reliable."

Leo Durocher

Manager • Brooklyn, N.L. • September 24, 1940

Leo Durocher, who hated taking orders from anyone, once followed the advice of a fan and nearly lost a ball game.

Going into the seventh inning at Ebbets Field, Leo's Brooklyn Dodgers were beating the New York Giants 5–0 behind the strong pitching of Whitlow Wyatt.

The fans were delighted, especially Hilda Chester, "the First Lady of Flatbush." As Brooklyn's most famous booster, she sat in the bleachers, ringing a cowbell and cheering on "Dem Bums" at almost every home game in the early 1940s.

During this particular Giants-Dodgers game, Hilda, who considered herself an expert on baseball, thought that Wyatt was losing his stuff and should be relieved. So she wrote a note to Leo telling him to get Hugh Casey, the team's best relief pitcher, warmed up and into the game. Before the top of the seventh inning was over, Hilda got the attention of Pete Reiser, Brooklyn's rookie center fielder, while he was still out in the field. She tossed him a wadded-up piece of paper and ordered him to give it to Durocher. Without reading the note, Reiser stuffed it in his back pocket.

When the inning was over, Reiser jogged toward the dugout, but first stopped off to speak briefly with Dodger president Larry MacPhail, who was sitting in a nearby box. Then Reiser went over to Leo and gave him the note.

After reading the message, Durocher had a puzzled look on his face. Then he walked over to Wyatt, who had pitched shutout ball for seven innings, and told him that his day's work was done. Durocher called in Casey to pitch the final two innings. Unfortunately, Casey didn't have it that day and was bombed for four runs in the eighth. The Dodgers barely held on for a 5–4 victory.

After the game, Leo, still fuming over the note's instructions which nearly cost his team a defeat, cornered Reiser and shouted, "Don't you, or anyone else, ever bring me a note from MacPhail."

"But, Mr. Durocher, that wasn't from MacPhail," explained the rookie.

"Then who in the hell gave it to you?"

"Hilda."

Durocher's jaw dropped. He spun on his heels and walked away, muttering to himself. Later, Leo told reporters, "I've heard of front-office interference, but how about me listening to that crazy dame with the cowbell!"

MASCOT MADNESS

*There are some things the world could do just fine without. War . . .
famine . . . pestilence . . . baseball mascots. Who needs them? Fans go
to the ball park to watch the game, not some waddling, squawking,
Sesame Street–type mutant. What's with all these overgrown chickens, parrots, and loons? Are they some new zoological species
waiting to be classified? For "The Tackiest Team Mascots," The Baseball Hall of SHAME inducts the following:*

The Baseball Bug

Mascot • Cleveland, A.L. • 1980–81

The Cleveland Indians crossed a giant baseball with a mutant insect and
created a mascot called the Baseball Bug. It was an idea whose time would
never come.

The Baseball Bug had a globe-shaped red body, wore a blue vest, and
sported antennae of springs with baseballs on the ends. It resembled no
insect that ever appeared in a biology book.

How could supposedly sane people come up with an oversized bug for a
mascot? To promote the game, the team had slogans like, "Catch Indian
fever." How do you get the fever? You get bitten by the Baseball Bug. Right,
and then you get ill knowing that your team created this sickening mascot.

Fans at Cleveland's Municipal Stadium wanted nothing to do with the bug.
They hurled not only obscenities at it, but also trash, soda, and even bats. It
made no difference to them that their mascot was the most overqualified
bug in history. Ron Cherneck, who cavorted in the ridiculous Baseball Bug
costume, had an MBA. He should have studied driver's education. On
Opening Day in 1981, he rode a motorcycle around the stadium—and promptly
fell off.

At least the Baseball Bug did one good thing. He managed to upset
Yankees owner George Steinbrenner by "mooning" the team. "I had a big

Indians body shirt on and it went down to about my knees on the costume," said Cherneck. "During a series with the Yankees, I got on top of their dugout and lifted the back of my shirt and bent over and 'mooned' the Yankees every time they struck out or did something bad in the field. The fans cheered me on. But Steinbrenner had no sense of humor. He filed a protest and I was ordered to stay off the dugout and off the field during all other Yankee games that year."

The Baseball Bug was simply following a legacy of incredibly ridiculous mascots. His predecessor was the Duck, some guy dressed up in a really quackers costume. The mascot had no name. The fans, however, had plenty of names for it. None of them is printable.

Rob Pike, who shares part of the blame for foisting the bug on the Cleveland spectators, said, "We were searching around for just the right mascot that would appeal to the fans because God knows the team wasn't doing much to please them.

"It was a nice try. But in retrospect, I have to admit that the idea of the Baseball Bug was pretty stupid." It sure was.

Schottzie

Mascot • Cincinnati, N.L. • 1985–present

Never in the history of baseball has a mascot gained the incredible power Schottzie wielded over a team.

While giving the appearance of a dumb, sad-faced 170-pound Saint Bernard, Schottzie in reality is a clever, conniving bitch. Here's the untold story.

Ever since her companion Marge Schott took over the presidency of the Cincinnati Reds in 1985 and made her the team mascot, Schottzie has managed to keep a leg up over everyone else on the team.

When Schott held a press conference announcing that Pete Rose was the new manager, Schottzie immediately threw her weight around. "Hey, Marge," Pete whispered during the conference, "Schottzie is sitting on my foot." Giving Pete a quick lesson about where he stood in the Reds' pecking order, Schott replied, "Tough, Pete."

Schottzie, the only dog in major league baseball to have her own air-conditioned office, has single-pawedly achieved a level of importance not known by even the team's superstars. In the 1986 Reds' press guide, Schottzie's picture and biography come right after Marge Schott's but before the bios of Pete Rose and general manager Bill Bergesch. Not only that but the Reds' ticket calendar does not have a single photo of a player, not even of Rose. Instead, there are twelve shots of Schottzie, including one in a Santa Claus outfit, another as Miss Liberty, and one as a valentine.

AP/Wide World Photos

It's all part of a shameless licensing and merchandising campaign that has overshadowed the public awareness of the Cincinnati players. Schottzie has been immortalized in floppy-eared hats, T-shirts, magnets, and stuffed animals, among other items.

Sales were boosted by her TV appearance on "Late Night with David Letterman" in New York. But she refused to take part in one of Letterman's favorite schticks on the show—stupid pet tricks. In a revealing comment before her appearance, Schott confessed to a reporter, "Schottzie doesn't do tricks. She might give you her paw. Now or then, she might run after a tennis ball and get it. But then, she might not. Her biggest trick is eating." Marge could say that again. Before one game, reporters marveled at the way Schottzie wolfed down a roast beef sandwich, a spinach soufflé, bratwurst, and potato chips.

There's no doubt that Marge Schott loves her dog very much. But Marge better be careful. Schottzie has her eyes set on taking over, according to insiders, who contend that a mishap involving the pair was no accident. In November 1985, while playing with Marge, the Saint Bernard backed her into a wall. Taken by surprise, Marge raised her arms and exposed her ribs to the huge dog. Schottzie then leaned against her mistress—and broke two of Marge's ribs.

Chief Noc-A-Homa

Mascot • Atlanta, N.L. • May 26, 1969

Chief Noc-A-Homa, the buckskin- and moccasin-clad mascot of the Atlanta Braves, fired up the crowd like never before. The chief accidentally set his tepee ablaze.

Before the start of every home game, Noc-A-Homa did a war dance on the mound and then ran out to his tepee beyond the left-field fence. Whenever a Brave hit a home run, the chief went into a celebration dance and set off a smoke bomb.

For two months, everything went according to script—until a night game against the St. Louis Cardinals. When Atlanta's Clete Boyer socked a round-tripper in the sixth inning, Noc-A-Homa slipped inside the tepee, lit the smoke bomb, stepped outside, and began his home run dance in front of 33,000 fans.

"Apparently, the smoke bomb got caught between the tepee pole and the canvas," he recalled. "The next thing I knew, the canvas caught on fire. I didn't think it would burn too fast, but it did.

"I tried to put out the fire. Beer, Coke, and every kind of beverage you could think of came pouring out of the stands. The grounds crew came running over to help out. One of them gave me a broom and I tried to beat out the fire. Instead, I knocked down one of the crew members. Eventually, we put out the fire with an extinguisher. I never heard the end of it."

The tepee was quickly replaced. Just before the start of the next game, the Braves players called Noc-A-Homa over and said, "Chief, we got a new uniform for you." Then they brought out a firefighter's suit complete with a big hat and boots and a little oxygen tank on the back.

From then on, the Indian mascot became a favorite target of the enemy bullpen, which was located right underneath the tepee. Players threw baseballs, clumps of Georgia clay, and ice at him. Once, the San Francisco Giants' bullpen crew blitzed the beleaguered chief with water balloons and a steady stream from a garden hose. In retaliation, Noc-A-Homa darted into his tepee and emerged with a thirty-pound fire extinguisher and covered the bullpen with foam.

During a game in 1971, Cardinals relief pitcher Moe Drabowsky tossed a stink bomb into the tepee. The chief staggered out, rubbing his eyes and holding his nose. Then the devilish Drabowsky lobbed a cherry bomb that exploded under Noc-A-Homa with such a bang that it sent the frightened chief jumping to new heights. Said St. Louis infielder Ted Sizemore, who witnessed the scene, "That Indian had to change loincloths between innings."

Twinkie the Loon

Mascot • Minnesota Twins • 1980–81

The Minnesota Twins didn't need any more clowns. They had enough of them in the starting lineup. Nevertheless, the front office brought in a new mascot to liven up the game—a jumbo-sized loon nicknamed Twinkie.

Local entertainer Al Johnson dressed in a costume that made him look like a ne'er-do-well brother-in-law of Big Bird. Twinkie the Loon—a weird representation of the state bird—had a unique rapport with the spectators. He juggled red plastic bats and made strange animals out of balloons. The fans responded with cute comments such as: "Down in front!" and "Get the hell outta the way!"

It was a loony idea from the start. The fans wanted Twinkie to just fly away. "There are some who look at me and you can just feel 'em saying, 'Get out of here,' " Twinkie told the press in his rookie year as a loon. "They look at me like I'm the Ayatollah Khomeini."

The life of the Twins' mascot was especially tough when dealing with fans of the visiting Milwaukee Brewers. "They were pushing me and yelling at me," said Twinkie. "I knew they were really mad when they started pouring beer on me. Nobody from Wisconsin throws beer away unless they really dislike you."

But getting doused with beer wasn't his worst experience. "The worst was when a Brewer fan came up and bit my beak and wouldn't let go."

To the fans, Twinkie became the symbol of second-class, second-division losers everywhere. Minnesotans let the team know exactly how they felt. Fans wrote in to the *St. Paul Pioneer Press* complaining about the loon. "I like loons generally, but they belong on lakes, not ball fields—unless they are right-handed, power-hitting loons who can bat .325 and hit 20 homers," wrote Toni Mennell, of Roseville.

Said Al Casazza, of Cottage Grove: "I've heard rumors that there are actually two Loons—one right-handed and one left-handed. [Manager] Gene Mauch has said that in the long run, his two-Loon platoon system will be better for the ball club. While one Loon works his way down the right-field line, the other goes toward left field. On days when one Loon is sick, the other can pinch-Loon without having to come in cold out of the loony bin."

The Twins had a better idea. They clipped Twinkie the Loon's wings for good by firing him.

SUBSTANDARD BEARERS

Baseball players set examples for kids, but, unfortunately, not all examples are good ones. Imagine if youngsters emulated some of the game's woeful "heroes," those rogues who seem to live each day in foul territory. Kids would learn everything from torching uniforms to peeing in public. For "The Sorriest Role Models for America's Youth," The Baseball Hall of SHAME inducts the following:

"The Tinkle Twins"
Don Mattingly   Dale Berra
First Baseman   Infielder
New York, A.L. • May 9–11, 1985

The New York Yankees were mortified by the leakiest infield ever. Not on the field but off it.

While on their first road trip in 1985 to Kansas City, Yankee infielders Don Mattingly and Dale Berra were arrested for peeing in public at a fashionable shopping center.

Although the charges against them were really quite piddling, the players' reputations were slightly yellowed. Imagine Dale, the son of Hall of Famer Yogi Berra, and Mattingly, 1985's American League MVP, being dubbed by the New York press as "The Tinkle Twins." What a pisser!

Of the pair, Mattingly was the first to expose himself to trouble when police saw him taking a leak at a street corner at the swank Country Club Plaza. Hustled off to the hoosegow, Don was given a municipal summons for indecent conduct and released on a signature bond. "I made a mistake," he said at the time, "but I don't think I will make it again. Now I just have to live it down."

Two nights later, it was Berra's turn to be caught with his pants down. Police spotted him watering a parking garage without a hose. In addition to a charge of indecent conduct, Dale was cited for assault after allegedly scuffling with the arresting officer. Berra was released on a $25 bond.

The incidents clearly angered Yankees owner George Steinbrenner, who fined the players $1,000 each. "I'm convinced it's embarrassing to these two young men," he said. "They were dead wrong."

When the Yankees visited Kansas City in 1986, Don made amends by playing in a benefit wheelchair softball game that helped the city's handicapped. Mattingly pitched and went 0–for–1.

There was one unsolved riddle to the double piddle. Both players were peeing in public right after leaving a restaurant owned by then Yankees coach Lou Piniella. That left fans pondering the question: Is there something wrong with Piniella's bathrooms?

John Lowenstein

Outfielder–Designated Hitter
Cleveland–Texas–Baltimore, A.L. • 1970–85

If a boy ever wants to make his mother scream in anguish, all he has to do is say, "Mom, when I grow up, I want to be just like John Lowenstein."

Steiner, as his teammates often called him, was born in the darkest corner of left field, spent his childhood in foul territory, and lasted sixteen years in the majors by riding the bench better than any other flake. Youngsters foolish enough to look up to him learned all about demanding more money for doing less, milking a crowd for sympathy, promoting apathy, and destroying birthday cakes.

In the fall of 1975, Lowenstein, then a backup player for the Cleveland Indians, gained notoriety by making the most unusual salary demand in baseball: "Play me or pay me."

He claimed that those who don't play regularly should be paid more for "the inconvenience." Explaining his wacky demand, Lowenstein told the press, "Playing irregularly is a far greater emotional strain than hearing the cheers and boos every day. There is a tendency to become a more irritable person. You begin to lose friends . . . and your body, not knowing what to expect, can suffer a heart seizure when suddenly called upon to play."

Steiner, a lifetime .255 hitter, insisted that general manager Phil Seghi "could set a precedent for the nation's economy and make history by paying me more for doing less." Seghi chose to decline this honor.

John said that being a benchwarmer cost him endorsements because "nobody wants to be identified with an employed spectator." He tried to get a shaving cream company to pay him for shaving off his mustache. "It was a Venezuelan shaving cream that nobody ever heard of." But the company never heard of Lowenstein and clipped his idea of an endorsement.

Who cared anyway? Certainly not the millions of people who supposedly belonged to the LAC—the Lowenstein Apathy Club. You automatically became a member if you were totally disinterested in Lowenstein.

He received hundreds of letters—many signed in invisible ink—pledging indifference about his career. Some fans promised to hold a day for him when the Indians were on the road. Occasionally, in the upper deck at Municipal Stadium, spectators hung a banner that read, "Hey, Steiner." It was followed by twenty feet of empty cloth.

At a time when ball clubs urged closer ties with the fans, John angered many spectators. He declined their requests for his autograph by claiming, "Sorry, I left it in the clubhouse."

But as a Baltimore Oriole, he won the fans over in June of 1980 when he put on a shameless performance at Memorial Stadium worthy of Sarah Bernhardt. Running from first to second in a game against the Oakland A's, Lowenstein was hit in the back of the neck by a thrown ball. He went down in a heap and appeared seriously injured.

"I just lay there pretending I was out cold," John recalled. "I had been waiting years for just such a situation. Everybody came running out and I could see through my eyelashes that the trainers, the manager, and the players were very concerned.

"Then they brought out the stretcher. About 35,000 people in the stands held their breath and it was so quiet that I figured they were praying that I was okay.

"As I was being carried off the field on the stretcher, there was this great hush. Just as they brought me near the dugout, I suddenly rose up with both fists clenched and let out a bloodcurdling yell. And the whole place just exploded. It was the loudest roar I've ever heard. It was simply an opportunity I couldn't pass up."

Lowenstein could never pass up the opportunity to conduct a zany examination of any birthday cake delivered to the clubhouse. "You never know what viral infections cakes may have," he explained. "I gave it the finger-plunge test. If it tasted very good, I left it alone." However, if the cake failed to meet Steiner's strict standards, he took a specially designed bat and smashed it. His teammates would chant, "Low, Low, Low" as he beat the cake into mush. The cake destruction cost him $5 every time. That's what he paid the clubhouse man to clean up the mess.

Doug Corbett

Pitcher • Minnesota, A.L. • May 18, 1980

Doug Corbett seemed like the kind of rookie kids wanted to emulate. In his first year in the bigs in 1980, the right-handed relief pitcher sported an impressive 8–6 record with 23 saves and a 1.99 ERA. He enjoyed a season that young fans dream about.

That's assuming, of course, they forgot the one mortifying moment when Corbett's cup didn't runneth over. It ran down his leg.

Pitching in Metropolitan Stadium against batter Paul Molitor of the Milwaukee Brewers, Corbett wound up and fired a fastball. He let it all hang out—in more ways than one. "The jockstrap broke and my cup went down my pants and was bulging at my knee," recalled Corbett. "I was turning as red as a beet.

"Fortunately, the pitch resulted in a ground ball and the third out of the inning so I was able to leave the field. But it wasn't easy trying to hide the fact that I had a cup protruding from my knee. I looked pretty odd stiff-legging it off the field like that. I'm just glad the people in the stands couldn't see how red my face was.

"I was wearing an old jockstrap because as a rookie I couldn't afford more than one a year. Now I make sure I have several new jockstraps. It could have been worse. What if my jock had broken at the start of the inning?"

Damaso Garcia

Second Baseman • Toronto, A.L. • May 14, 1986

As part of a joint fire-safety campaign with the Toronto Blue Jays, the Ontario Association of Fire Chiefs had just released a baseball card of Damaso Garcia with a fire-prevention tip on the back.

The timing couldn't have been worse.

His reputation as fire-safety promoter went up in smoke following a game against the Athletics in Oakland. The star second baseman had committed a damaging error that let in the go-ahead run in the Blue Jays' 9–4 loss. Afterward, the rest of his teammates were hurriedly packing for the flight home to Toronto, but Garcia was still smoldering over his fielding miscue. He chose not to vent his frustration the typical way by smashing water coolers, tearing up a bat rack, or destroying a toilet. Instead, he went into the bathroom, poured alcohol over his uniform, and torched it.

The incendiary act has been practiced occasionally in baseball. In fact, a few weeks earlier, Chicago White Sox pitcher Bob James became a firebug. Disgusted with his performance on the mound, James stalked into the clubhouse and burned his entire uniform, including his jockstrap.

What made Garcia's flare-up so shameful was his failure to practice what he preached. On the back of his special baseball card, he had offered this fire-safety tip: "Keep your infield free of errors. Remove all rubbish from your basement or attic." He certainly didn't keep his infield free of errors and he didn't remove the rubbish, which in this case was the charred remains of his uniform.

What did the fire chiefs' association have to say? In answer to the burning question of the day, association president Dave Kemp admitted, "It's kind of embarrassing for us to have one of our spokesmen for fire prevention pull a stunt like that."

Dock Ellis

Pitcher • Pittsburgh, N.L. • July–August, 1973

Pitcher Dock Ellis threw manhood a curve by sporting curlers in his hair during pre-game workouts.

Much to the dismay of Pittsburgh fans, one of their favorite pitchers had suddenly become the darling of America's hairdressers.

Hurlers are a strange breed anyway. One of their main pursuits is looking for a new pitch. For Dock, it was pitching a new look.

It usually got him into hairy situations. In 1972, he displayed the full afro look and was mistaken for a fan. When Ellis failed to produce proper

identification at the players' gate in Cincinnati and tried to force his way in, he was maced by a Riverfront Stadium guard. "Maybe I looked too wild to be a ball player," said Dock after the incident. "I had just had my hair blown out."

Ellis caused permanent waves in 1973 during a pre-game workout at Wrigley Field in Chicago. That's where he introduced his latest style by striding out to the bullpen wearing white hair curlers. When a fan asked him, "What's up, Dock?" Ellis simply pointed to his "do."

When a wire service photo of Ellis in curlers was published in newspapers across the country, it made the hair of Pirate officials stand on end. General manager Joe Brown said the curlers were unbecoming to a major leaguer and banned Ellis from wearing them in pre-game workouts. "I know the orders came from [commissioner] Bowie Kuhn and I don't like it," declared the pitcher. "They didn't put any orders about [Yankees star] Joe Pepitone when he wore a hairpiece down to his shoulders."

Reluctantly, Dock shelved the curlers. Why would a major league ball player wear curlers in public? Only his hairdresser knows for sure.

DIAMOND DEBACLES

Youngsters try to copy every move the superstars make on the field so they can grow up and become major leaguers, too. But sometimes, the players in the bigs perform as though they are trying to imitate the kids in the sandlots. The sport has been blighted by misplays so farcical that there's talk the commissioner's office plans to destroy all film and video tape of these absurd moments. For "Little League Plays Committed by Big League Players," The Baseball Hall of SHAME inducts the following:

Cleveland Indians

August 10, 1978

No infield pop-up was ever more shamefully misplayed than the one lofted by Butch Hobson of the Boston Red Sox. The Cleveland Indians botched up the play so badly it couldn't even be repeated on instant replay.

In the bottom of the 13th inning at Fenway Park, the Indians held a 5–4 lead when Hobson stepped to the plate as Boston's lead-off batter. Butch hit a high, lazy pop-up toward second, a seemingly routine out. But then, nothing has ever been routine for the Indians—except losing.

Second baseman Duane Kuiper camped under the ball. Suddenly, he began to stagger when he momentarily lost the ball in the late-afternoon sun. First baseman Andre Thornton then raced over to help out while the hustling Hobson charged around first and steamed toward second in the one-in-a-million chance that the ball would fall safely.

At the last second, Kuiper spotted the descending ball and moved over to catch it. Unfortunately, he did this at the very moment that Thornton also was reaching out for the ball. The resulting collision caused Thornton to drop the ball, and it rolled over toward first.

With a quick glance over his shoulder, Hobson saw that the Indians had screwed up, so he took off for third. Catcher Bo Diaz, who had backed up the play at first, retrieved the ball and fired it to third in an attempt to nail Hobson. But Diaz's throw sailed over the third baseman's head and bounced down the left-field line.

Hobson, who had slid into third, scrambled to his feet and decided there was no sense stopping now since the Indians were on a roll. While Hobson headed for home, left fielder John Grubb picked up the errant throw and had plenty of time to throw out Hobson at the plate—but Grubb couldn't get the ball out of his glove! Hobson slid across home with a belly flop to tie the score. The Indians never recovered. "The Hobson Hustle," as the Boston faithful fondly called it, was followed by a double and a single for a 6–5 Cleveland loss.

After the game, Indians manager Jeff Torborg talked with numbing bewilderment. "In all my years in baseball, I have never seen a play like that. How can a man get four bases on an infield pop?" Simple. Play the Cleveland Indians.

Detroit Tigers

May 12, 1976

On their zaniest day, not even baseball clowns Al Schacht and Max Patkin could have pulled off the comedy routine that the Detroit Tigers staged at Yankee Stadium.

The curtain on this farce was raised in the fourth inning with one out and New York runners Jim Mason and Mickey Rivers at second and first respectively. Batter Roy White then hit a catchable drive toward center fielder Ron LeFlore.

Mason, who believed there were two outs, didn't wait to see whether or not the ball would be caught and ran blithely toward third. Coach Dick Howser waved frantically at him to stop and go back. But then LeFlore, who in the first inning had dropped a fly ball for an error that led to three unearned runs, muffed this one, too. By this time, Mason had stumbled rounding third base. "I fell when I tried to stop," Mason explained sheepishly. "Dick stuck his hands up and I didn't understand why, but I figured I had better stop. Then when LeFlore dropped the ball, Dick told me to keep going. I came out smelling like a rose."

Not quite. LeFlore recovered the ball quickly and fired it home where catcher John Wockenfuss deftly tagged Mason out. But Wockenfuss, wrongly thinking there were three outs, nonchalantly rolled the ball toward the mound. Rivers, who had scampered all the way to third base by this time, kept on running and came in to score. "I just wasn't thinking correctly," the catcher admitted. "Everything was right, except that Ron didn't catch the ball. It didn't register that he had dropped it. I was thinking double play. I just blew it, plain and simple."

Detroit pitcher Bill Laxton, who had gone toward the plate to back up the throw from LeFlore, gasped when Wockenfuss rolled the ball toward the mound. Laxton broke for the ball and, frustrated that he couldn't get Rivers, threw toward third where White—who started the whole mess—was headed. Naturally, the throw sailed past third and into left field. White scored, too, with what proved to be the winning run in a 7–6 New York victory.

Since there were no more Yankees on base, several Tigers were able to surround the ball and subdue it. They could only shudder at what they had just witnessed. Here's the score-book account of White's progress around the bases on what should have been a routine fly out: reached first on the center fielder's error, went to second on the throw-in, made it to third on the catcher's miscue, and scored on the pitcher's wild peg. Three runs and three errors on one play!

White wasn't quite sure what had happened until the inning was over and he saw a taped replay of the incident on the huge Yankee Stadium scoreboard. The crowd of 14,575 roared with laughter during the replay but it was no laughing matter in the Detroit dugout.

"I saw it once," muttered Tigers manager Ralph Houk, "and I don't need to look at it again."

Texas Rangers

June 16, 1986

Texas Rangers knuckleballer Charlie Hough was only two outs away from a no-hit, shutout victory. But from then on, every Ranger who touched the ball screwed up in the most disgraceful windup ever to a brilliantly pitched game. Hough lost the no-hitter, the shutout, and the victory.

Twirling against the California Angels in Anaheim Stadium, Hough baffled batters all night with his 70 mph fluttering pitch. But with one out in the bottom of the ninth in a 1–0 nail-biter, it was his own team who looked baffled.

The first sign of trouble came when Angels batter Jack Howell hit a fly ball down the left-field line. George Wright, who had just replaced Gary Ward in left for defensive purposes, overran the ball and it bounced off the heel of his glove for a three-base error.

Instead of two outs and no one on base, the Angels had the tying run on third and only one out. Hough still had to get two more outs to earn his no-hitter. But the blunder really shook him up. Before he had time to settle down, Hough gave up California's only hit of the night, a single by rookie Wally Joyner that not only ruined the no-hitter but tied the score at 1–1.

Fate wasn't through dumping on Hough. One of his knuckleballs skipped past catcher Orlando Mercado for a passed ball. Joyner raced to second base, representing the winning run. But Hough bore down and struck out the batter before intentionally walking Reggie Jackson.

With two on and two out, Hough worked the count on George Hendrick to 3–and–2. Then the hurler threw another floater and Hendrick swung and missed for the third out. But wait. Mercado once again couldn't handle the pitch and the ball rolled to the backstop.

By the time Mercado tracked down the ball, he realized he had no play at first base. He also realized the Rangers were about to blow the game because Joyner was racing around third and heading for the plate. "I saw Wally coming and knew that was our only play," recalled Mercado. But there was no play because Hough was still standing on the mound shell-shocked by all the bad luck. Instead of covering the plate, Hough watched Joyner joyfully cross home with the winning run.

"Losing is an empty feeling," said Hough. "Orlando and I were both standing there looking like jerks when it was over."

Los Angeles Dodgers and San Francisco Giants

June 2, 1961

For sustained confusion, frustration, craziness, and goofiness, no inning can match the last half of the ninth of a wild game between the visiting San Francisco Giants and the Los Angeles Dodgers.

It was as if the teams were playing out a bizarre script written jointly by Franz Kafka and Woody Allen.

"At one time, I had no notion of what was going on," admitted Dodgers manager Walter Alston.

Some of the lowlights: a Dodger was ejected for protesting a call on a play that never happened, a pinch runner ran back to an already-occupied base, and relief pitchers were brought in just to *walk* batters.

It all started when Willie Davis led off the nutty half inning with a home run that tied the score at 2–2. When pitcher Bobby Bolin ran the count on the next batter, Wally Moon, to 3–and–1, Giants manager Alvin Dark brought in reliever Billy O'Dell. O'Dell threw one pitch for a ball. Moon walked. And so did O'Dell—to the showers. He was replaced by Stu Miller.

Next up was Tommy Davis, who attempted a sacrifice bunt down the first-base line. It was a typical play—for the Twilight Zone. Catcher Hobie Landrith sprang from behind the plate and fired the ball to shortstop José Pagan at second where umpire Augie Donatelli called the sliding Moon out.

Wally exploded in rage and carried on a heated belly-to-belly argument with Donatelli that looked like the two were bumping to the rhythm of a conga beat. Finally, Moon pushed Donatelli too far and the ump threw him out of the game.

Meanwhile, back at home plate, Landrith and umpire Ken Burkhart were having a little to-do of their own. Incredibly, Burkhart had declared Tommy Davis's sacrifice bunt foul! That meant all of Moon's arguing was needless. Nevertheless, his ejection still held. So Bob Aspromonte was sent to first as a pinch runner for the banished Moon.

Davis tried bunting again, and, fortunately for the Dodgers, he succeeded. Unfortunately for the Giants, first baseman Willie McCovey booted the ball. Davis and Aspromonte were safe at first and second respectively.

Sensing that this inning had a shot for the Hall of Shame, fans edged forward in their seats waiting for something else weird to happen. They didn't have to wait long. While working on the next batter, Norm Larker, Stu Miller pitched out and the Dodgers' Sleeping Beauty, Aspromonte, clearly was trapped off second. Aspromonte headed for third and then turned around and ran back to second base. However, there was a slight problem. Teammate Tommy Davis was already standing there. When Davis had seen Aspromonte scamper toward third, he had chugged into second. Now two confused Dodgers were standing on the same base. Meanwhile, catcher Hobie Landrith had run all the way out to second and tagged them both just to be sure somebody was out. Even though Aspromonte hadn't shown much interest in owning second, the rules stated that he had possession. So, through no fault of his own, Davis was called out. Miller then walked Larker and coaxed Daryl Spencer to hit into a force-out at second. It looked like normalcy had finally returned to the game. It hadn't.

With Dodger runners at first and third and two out, left-handed batter Norm Sherry was sent up to pinch-hit for Johnny Roseboro. So Dark countered by summoning southpaw Mike McCormick to the mound. A smart piece of strategy? That depends. McCormick did exactly what Dark ordered him to do—he intentionally walked Sherry to load the bases. Then Dark lifted the hurler for righty Eddie Fisher.

That's because Alston was sending right-handed Frank Howard up as another pinch hitter. However, when Fisher began warming up, Alston told Howard to forget it and replaced him with left-handed Duke Snider, a pinch hitter for the pinch hitter. The strategy failed. Snider lined the first pitch to center field for the third out. The crazy inning was finally over.

"I saw it, but I don't believe it," reported veteran Giants broadcaster Russ Hodges. "Thirty minutes to get three outs—and one run is scored."

The insanity carried over into the next and final inning. In the bottom of the tenth with the bases loaded, Dodgers hitter Tommy Davis blasted a ball into the left-field stands for a game-winning grand slam. However, it almost wasn't a homer. The runner on first, Bob Aspromonte—the guy who had retreated from near third to second in the previous inning—jauntily headed for the dugout after Davis's shot cleared the fence. Only the restraining hands of first base coach Pete Reiser saved Aspromonte from being passed on the base path by Davis—a blunder that would have turned the grand slammer into a single.

Said Alvin Dark, "I've never seen anything like it. I never want to again."

Cincinnati Reds

August 10, 1977

"If Branch Rickey had been alive today and seen that play, it would've killed him," lamented Sparky Anderson, shortly after witnessing the most shameful rundown in major league history.

Anderson, manager of the Cincinnati Reds and a disciple of Rickey, the legendary baseball mentor, barely survived the play himself. "We pick a guy off base and he beats us. That can't happen."

But it did happen. Every Reds infielder was involved in the rundown, yet they failed to catch and tag out the trapped runner.

In the third inning of a critical game between the second-place Reds and first-place Dodgers in Los Angeles, Cincy pitcher Fred Norman spotted L.A. base runner Davey Lopes napping off first base. Norman fired over to first baseman Dan Driessen for what should have been a simple pickoff play.

But Lopes sped off toward second and Driessen, failing to chase him long enough, threw too early to second baseman Joe Morgan. Lopes put on the brakes and headed back toward first. This time it was Morgan who threw too soon. When Driessen caught Morgan's return toss, Lopes went into reverse, so Driessen shoveled the ball—again, too early—to shortstop Dave Concepcion. The fugitive Lopes continued to skitter between the two bases as Concepcion tossed the ball to Morgan. By now third baseman Pete Rose joined in the rundown odyssey by guarding second base. Morgan then flipped the ball underhanded and so low to Rose that it actually rolled the last few feet. It didn't much matter. Rose bobbled the ball anyway.

Here's the lowdown on the rundown: the Reds made six throws in all, yet they not only failed to tag Lopes, they allowed him to advance a base. Everyone in the infield except catcher Johnny Bench had handled the ball, and still Lopes reached second safely.

From there, Lopes was sacrificed to third by Bill Russell and brought home by Reggie Smith's single to left. Lopes scored the game's only run, an unearned one.

"You don't see a rundown that bad in Class-A ball," Anderson muttered angrily. "I want to hang my head somewhere and not let anyone see me. I don't want to be out socially. That's how disgraced I feel. I just want to be in dark alleys."

HEAVE HO-HO'S

Although umpires don't see all the things they should, they usually hear all the things they shouldn't. What usually follows is a heated argument that often ends when the arbiter thumbs his antagonist out of the game. However, this ritual sometimes takes a bizarre twist and ends up looking like a Barnum & Bailey sideshow. For "The Most Inglorious Ejections from a Game," The Baseball Hall of SHAME inducts the following:

Edd Roush

Outfielder • Cincinnati, N.L. • June 8, 1920

Edd Roush never said a word. He never made a gesture. Yet he was ejected from a game for conduct unbecoming a professional baseball player.

Roush was given the boot for taking a nap in center field!

In the eighth inning of a game between the New York Giants and Cincinnati Reds at the Polo Grounds, Giants batter George Burns slapped a grounder over third base down the left-field line. Umpire Barry McCormack called the ball fair, whereupon Reds catcher Ivy Wingo tossed his glove in the air in protest. McCormack did one better. The ump tossed his mask and his thumb in the air, signaling Wingo to the showers. Meanwhile, Burns ended up at third.

After calling time, the entire Reds infield swooped in on McCormack like a SWAT team and heatedly argued that it was a foul ball. While the battle raged at home plate, Roush became bored. So he placed his glove and cap on the ground and used them as a pillow while he stretched out in center field for a short snooze. He quickly fell into a deep sleep.

Edd slumbered through the stormy dispute and all its fury: the rantings of third baseman Heinie Groh; the Spanish obscenities uttered by pitcher Dolph Luque; the pleadings of Reds manager Pat Moran; and the wild departure of

Wingo, who threw his catching gear all over the field as he headed for the dugout.

Once the squabble ended, McCormack sent the Reds back to their positions and was just about ready to shout, "Play ball!" when he noticed that Roush was using center field as a sofa. Teammates yelled at Edd to get up, but their calls failed to rouse him. Finally, Heinie Groh raced out to center and managed to awaken the team's Rip Van Winkle. But by then, it was too late. When Roush opened his eyes, the first sight he saw was McCormack's thumb. The ejection immediately woke up Edd's temper and the heretofore dozing player launched into a tirade against the umpire. Roush, who wanted to duke it out with McCormack, was restrained by his teammates, who eventually ushered him to the dugout.

Manager Pat Moran couldn't understand why a player should be thrown out of a game simply for taking a nap in the outfield. "A lot of players have been caught sleeping on plays and they don't get the boot," he complained.

Frank Lucchesi

Manager • Philadelphia, N.L. • June 27, 1970

Frank Lucchesi was given the old heave-ho for staging a sit-in demonstration.

It happened during his rookie year as manager of the Philadelphia Phillies. Lucchesi, whose rantings and ravings against umpires in the minors were legendary, had finally argued his way up to the bigs. When he was nailed with his first major league ejection, Frank handled it with the class of a true Hall of Shamer.

In the bottom of the eighth inning of a game between the visiting Phils and the St. Louis Cardinals, the Cards' Jim Beauchamp swatted a tie-breaking homer. Immediately, Lucchesi bounded out of the dugout to protest. He argued that a fan had leaned out of the bleachers in right center and touched the ball below the yellow home run line. Umpire Tony Venzon, who made the call, stuck by his ruling.

Frank decided to take a new tack. He stamped his feet, threw his cap, pounded his fist into his palm, swore a blue streak, and kicked clouds of dust around the infield.

He didn't get anywhere with Venzon, so he tried pleading. "Just ask one of the other umpires because maybe you didn't see it well enough," Lucchesi asked. When the ump refused, the stormy manager replied defiantly, "Well, if you're not going to ask them, I'm not leaving." With that said, Frank anchored his butt on second base, turned his hat around, and folded his arms, looking like an angry Sitting Bull in double-knit gray.

"You're outta the game!" thundered Venzon. "Now get outta here!"

"I'm not leaving," said the stubborn Lucchesi.

After one long minute, Venzon said, "Frank, if you don't leave, we're going to forfeit the game. You have thirty seconds to get out and I'm counting, one ... two ... three ..."

When Venzon reached twenty-seven, Lucchesi figured it was time to split. He stomped off the field to the derisive cheers of the St. Louis fans. The moment he walked into the clubhouse, Frank received a long-distance phone call from Phillies general manager John Flynn, who had been watching the game on TV back in Philadelphia. Flynn told him, "That was quite a show you put on, but you don't do that in the big leagues."

Nevertheless, Lucchesi continued to play out his dramas on the field. Performing before a record crowd of 57,000 in Philly in May 1972, the tempestuous skipper put on a wild dirt-kicking act after getting the thumb from umpire Harry Wendlestedt. The ump calmly watched Frank's antics, then applauded politely and walked away. It was a devastating putdown.

At least Lucchesi's animated squabbles with the umps in the minors were appreciated. Once during a game in Denver, Frank was so teed off over his ejection that he yanked up the second base bag only to be chased by the umpire into the outfield. Cornered in right field, Lucchesi refused to give up the base. Instead, he threw it up into the bleachers.

In 1963 when he managed in Little Rock, Frank was thrown out of a game by an umpire who told him, "Let me give you some advice: keep your mouth shut." Lucchesi took the words to heart. Before the start of the next game, he delivered the lineup card at home plate with his mouth taped closed.

That same year, in Syracuse, Frank was tossed out of another game, but he was determined to watch the action anyway. Rather than go to the clubhouse, he climbed a light tower behind the outfield fence. When the umpires spotted him, they ordered him down. "I told them I was out of the park and I wasn't moving," Lucchesi recalled. "But the plate umpire said he'd give me one minute or he'd forfeit the game. I decided to get down but when I looked at the ground below, I suddenly realized I was afraid of heights and I was too scared to move. My team almost lost on a forfeit."

Perhaps Frank's most ignominious ejection came in 1973, a year after he was fired by the Phils. While managing in Oklahoma City, Lucchesi was so incensed over a disputed call that he kicked dirt on umpire Dale Ford's shoes. Then Frank dropped to his knees and piled a mound of dirt on home plate, patting it with a flourish. He was suspended for one game and fined $100. On the day of his punishment, club officials received a flowered wreath from a fan with this message: "Perhaps on Memorial Day, some understanding sports fan will place the wreath on the site where Mr. Lucchesi buried home plate."

Ron Fairly

First Baseman • California, A.L. • July 1, 1978

Ron Fairly turned a fairly routine play into a Fairly shameful ejection.

It happened when the California Angels were in the thick of the AL West pennant race and playing in front of a packed house at Anaheim Stadium against the Texas Rangers.

With one out and his team trailing 6–3 in the bottom of the eighth inning, Fairly was on first base when teammate Bobby Grich rapped a line drive that was snared by third baseman Toby Harrah. Ron, who took off with the crack of the bat, put on the skids.

But when he tried to reverse directions, Fairly fell flat on his face on the base path and then watched sheepishly as Harrah threw to first to double him up. Ron lay there and reflected on how a twenty-one-year veteran could so carelessly take his team out of a rally in a game they were losing.

That wasn't his only mistake. While still sprawled out on the ground, Fairly grabbed a handful of dirt and, in disgust, flipped it back over his head.

It wasn't Ron's lucky day. The dirt landed on the head and shoulders of first base umpire Terry Cooney. As the arbiter brushed the dirt off with one hand, he thumbed Fairly out of the game with the other.

Afterward, Ron was seen reading a book entitled *How to Get Through Your Struggles* by Oral Roberts.

Dick Drott

Pitcher • Chicago, N.L. • April 27, 1957

When Dick Drott tried to play nurse, he was thumbed out of the game by an ill-humored umpire.

Drott, a rookie sensation with the Chicago Cubs, was in the dugout watching his roommate, pitcher Moe Drabowsky, bat against Joe Nuxhall of the Cincinnati Reds. Moe worked a 2–2 count before Nuxhall threw a curve that broke sharply and struck Drabowsky on the foot. The batter looked for sympathy but found none on the stoic face of home plate umpire Stan Landes. So Moe launched into a performance worthy of an Oscar by crumpling to the ground and writhing in pain.

Drott decided that he couldn't just sit there and watch his teammate roll in the dirt in agony. As luck would have it, a crippled singer had sung the national anthem before the start of the game and was sitting in a front-row box seat next to the Cubs' dugout. Her wheelchair was by her side.

"Okay if I borrow it?" Dick asked her. Then, before hearing her answer, he grabbed the wheelchair and rolled it up to home plate. "Roomie," he said to his injured comrade, "get in the wheelchair and I'll give you a ride to first base."

That seemed like a terrific idea to Moe, but not to Landes. "What the hell are you doing?" the ump shouted at Drott.

"I'm only trying to help my roommate," Dick replied with a straight face. "He's hurt and he could use a hand."

Drabowsky did not get a hand, but Drott did get the thumb. "You're out of the game!" declared the unamused Landes. "And take that damn wheelchair with you!"

A few days later, Drott received a letter from Warren Giles, then president of the National League. "Warren indicated that he didn't know if Dick was trying to make a travesty of the game or if he really had my welfare at heart," recalled Drabowsky. "Not knowing what Dick's motives were, Warren was reluctant to fine him. However, he did tell Dick that such behavior would not be condoned in the future.

"I've seen a lot of crazy things in my seventeen years in the majors, but that was really one of the funniest things I ever saw—and I didn't even pull it."

Dummy Taylor

Pitcher • New York, N.L.; Cleveland, A.L. • 1900–08

Dummy Taylor was a deaf-mute—yet he still managed to get thrown out of games for "talking back" to the umpire.

Taylor didn't let his disability stop him from winning games or aggravating the men in blue. As a workhorse for the Giants, Taylor recorded 116 major league victories, including 21 in 1904 when he helped his team win its first pennant.

Although he couldn't speak or hear a word, Dummy became one of the most adroit umpire-baiters in the majors. He loved nothing better than to tell an arbiter off in sign language. For years, he got away with it because no one could "read" his fingers. He always stood at the end of the Giants' bench—even on days he was pitching—and joined in needling the umpires with finger signs, gestures, and looks of disdain. On the mound, Dummy was always arguing over balls and strikes. If he thought the umpire was wrong, Taylor would take off his glove, throw it on the ground, and trample it to show his utter disgust.

In 1902, when he pitched briefly for Cleveland, Dummy was given his first heave-ho. Throughout the game, Taylor was silently complaining about the ump's calls on balls and strikes. Dummy's lips moved continuously but the umpire ignored him. Finally, Taylor strode to the plate, stuck out his chin, and framed his words slowly and distinctly. The ump watched Dummy's lips for about thirty seconds and then waved him out of the game.

Afterward, the ump told reporters, "Even if I wasn't a good lip reader, I knew Taylor wasn't saying his prayers. For a guy who can't hear, he's picked up some nasty words. Why, he actually called me some names I'd never heard before."

Dummy enjoyed getting umpire Hank O'Day's goat. One afternoon, the Giants were playing under protest because it was raining and O'Day had refused to call the game. Taylor decided to show up the umpire. The pitcher went into the clubhouse and borrowed a pair of tall rubber boots from the groundskeeper. He carried these to the coaching box and placed them in an upright position while O'Day's back was turned. When O'Day spotted the boots, he knew it had to be the handiwork of Dummy Taylor. The ump threw him out of the game and had him fined.

From then on, Taylor and O'Day carried on a simmering feud. Time and again, Dummy would dress down the ump in sign language—with total impunity. O'Day was getting steamed and vowed to get even one day.

Finally, the day came. From the pitching mound in the middle of a game, Taylor let his fingers do the talking as he berated O'Day over a call. The arbiter's eyes never left Dummy's hands. When the pitcher finished his silent tirade, he gave O'Day a smug grin. But then to Taylor's shock, he saw the ump sign with his hands. "You go to the clubhouse. Pay $25." Surprised and deflated, Dummy left the field.

After the game, Taylor discovered that O'Day had learned sign language from a deaf relative. "Listen, smart guy," O'Day told him. "I've spent all my spare time this week learning your language. You can't call me a blind bat anymore."

Eddie Kasko

Manager • Boston, A.L. • July 7, 1972

Eddie Kasko was booted out of a game for lying down on the job—he faked a faint while protesting an umpire's call.

Kasko's swoon came in the ninth inning of a game between his visiting Boston Red Sox and the California Angels. With Boston leading 3–2 and Ben Oglivie on third base, Luis Tiant hit a grounder to shortstop Leo Cardenas, who fired to catcher Jeff Torborg to try to nail Oglivie at the plate. As Torborg was about to make the tag, Oglivie sidestepped him and then slid across the plate for what seemed like an insurance run.

Torborg and Angels manager Del Rice argued heatedly that Oglivie had run out of the base line. Plate umpire Hank Morganweek said no, but then huddled with crew chief John Rice, who was working at second base. Eventually, the umps reversed the decision and called Oglivie out. Kasko exploded from the dugout.

Turning his wrath on John Rice, Kasko shouted, "I don't believe this, John! Are you standing there telling me that even though you were on the outside part of the infield by second base, you saw the play at home plate better than Morganweek?"

The ump replied, "Yeah, that's exactly what I'm telling you."

Kasko was so upset he didn't know what to say. But he felt obligated to make a statement of some sort—so he keeled over backward on the grass as if he had fainted from disbelief over the call. At first, the umps were irritated over Kasko's showboating. But when he lay there spread-eagled, flat on his back for nearly a minute, they became alarmed.

"My God, he's had a heart attack!" shouted Rice. "Get a doctor out here!" But as the ump bent over, he saw Kasko open his eyes and grin. "Never mind the doctor," Rice said to his colleagues. Then, staring down at the prone manager, the ump bellowed, "You're out of the game!"

"For what?" Kasko asked.

"For fainting."

Kasko meekly left the field—but the umpires hadn't heard the last of him. In true Hall of SHAME style, Kasko managed to get ejected twice in the same game.

After the Angels tied the score at 3–3, Bosox utility man Phil Gagliano started mouthing off to Morganweek in the top of the tenth inning. Kasko, who now was watching the game from the tunnel leading to the clubhouse, charged out onto the field to protect his player from getting booted.

Rice immediately ran in from his position near second, confronted Kasko, and said, "I don't know if you remember it or not, but while you were passed out in the last inning, I threw you out. So get out of here!"

Norman "The Tabasco Kid" Elberfeld

Shortstop • New York, A.L. • September 3, 1906

Kid Elberfeld was dragged off the field kicking and screaming by a squad of policemen in the most disgraceful ejection ever witnessed on a major league diamond.

There was good reason why the New York Yankees shortstop was called "The Tabasco Kid." Although he was only 5-feet, 5-inches tall and weighed 135 pounds, Elberfeld had a king-size temper—hotter than a jalapeño—that labeled him the bad boy of baseball.

His most deplorable heave-ho came during the thick of the 1906 pennant race in the first game of a doubleheader against the visiting Philadelphia Athletics. In the top of the ninth inning of a 3–3 tie, A's runner Danny Murphy stole third base on a close play. Immediately, the Yankees surrounded umpire Francis O'Loughlin and protested the call. He quickly silenced them all—except for The Tabasco Kid.

Elberfeld approached the ump with his fists raised, but O'Loughlin disdainfully waved him away. The gesture infuriated the Kid, who rushed at the arbiter and attempted to kick him. O'Loughlin dodged him with the skill of a bullfighter and then, in the same motion, gave Elberfeld the thumb. In retaliation, the Kid gave O'Loughlin the finger. Wanting further vengeance, the wrathful player chased the ump all over the infield, trying six futile times to kick him in the butt and spike him in the foot.

When the alarmed umpire finally appealed to the police for help, three cops raced out onto the field and grabbed Elberfeld. Cursing at the top of his lungs, he was hustled off to the dugout while the 20,000 fans at New York's Hilltop Park jeered him.

O'Loughlin refused to allow the game to continue until the Kid was removed from the ball park. This only enraged Elberfeld more. Breaking free from the policemen's grasp, he charged after the umpire again. Teammate Al Orth tried to restrain him, but even though Orth had a seven-inch, sixty-five-pound advantage over the Kid, the furious Elberfeld still knocked Orth down and continued his mad rush toward O'Loughlin.

Once again, the beleaguered umpire was forced to run for his life until the cops recaptured the crazed player and hauled him off the field for the second time. When the Kid was brought to the players' gate, he wouldn't budge any further. Meanwhile, New York manager Clark Griffith feared the game would be forfeited because play had been held up for so long. Griffith ran up to Elberfeld and threatened to kick him off the team if he didn't leave. Reluctantly, the Kid finally shuffled off to the clubhouse with boos and hisses from the crowd still ringing in his ears.

TURNSTILE TURNOFFS

Baseball teams enjoy spreading cheer—and filling seats—by offer-ing gimmicks, giveaways, and lots of hoopla at games. These ball park promotions are designed to give fans more than their money's worth. But sometimes these marketing schemes give teams much more than they bargained for. For "Ball Park Promotions That Backfired," The Baseball Hall of SHAME inducts the following:

Reggie Candy Bar Day

Yankee Stadium • April 13, 1978
County Stadium • July 27, 1978

It seemed like a simple enough promotion. Give out free Reggie Bars—the candy that Reggie Jackson finally convinced someone to name after him—to the fans. But twice the promotion turned out nuttier than the confection itself.

For years, Jackson had been bragging that he was so great someone should name a candy bar after him. Standard Brands Confectionery Division finally broke down and did. For reasons known only to himself, Jackson had chosen to be immortalized in chewy chocolate and nuts.

To promote Reggie—both the candy bar and the player—all 44,667 fans at the New York Yankees' home opener in 1978 were given a free Reggie Bar. Jackson, always one to seize the moment, blasted a three-run homer in the first inning. As he trotted around the bases, he was suddenly showered not only with cheers but also Reggie Bars—from the bleachers, the mezzanine, the box seats, and the grandstands. The field was littered with Reggie Bars, forcing the umpires to call time while the grounds crew scooped up thousands upon thousands of candy bars.

After the game, won by the Yanks 4–2, Chicago White Sox manager Bob Lemon said, "How great a tasting candy bar could it be if they throw it instead of eat it?"

Three months later, plans for another Reggie Bar day turned sour. The Milwaukee Brewers intended to give away 50,000 of the confections right after the July 27 game with the Yankees at County Stadium. However, an ugly incident during the contest changed their minds.

After Brewers pitcher Mike Caldwell brushed back Jackson with a pitch, Reggie popped out. Fuming mad, Jackson threw his bat toward the mound. When Caldwell picked up the bat and tried to break it, Jackson charged the mound and grabbed the pitcher by the throat. That triggered a bench-clearing brawl. Milwaukee director of marketing Dick Hackett decided then and there not to pass out the Reggie Bars after the game. It would have been in bad taste.

Fourth of July Celebration

Atlanta Stadium • July 5, 1985

The Atlanta Braves' Independence Day fireworks show lit up more than just the sky. It sparked a blaze of alarm from stadium neighbors who thought they were being bombed.

Perhaps it had something to do with the time. Braves' management thoughtlessly set off the booming Fourth of July pyrotechnic display at *4:01* A.M. *on July 5.*

In all fairness, the Braves didn't plan on triggering the fireworks at such a wee hour of the morning. The team had promised the 44,947 fans who arrived at Atlanta Stadium a spectacular sky show after the night game with the New York Mets—but unfortunately, the game went on and on and on.

It turned into a record-setting marathon contest featuring an eighty-four-minute rain delay at the start of the game and another forty-one-minute interruption in the third inning. Making this a long night's journey into day was the game itself, a 19-inning affair that lasted six hours and ten minutes before the Mets won, 16–13.

When the game mercifully ended at 3:55 A.M.—the latest finish in major league history—only about 8,000 hardy souls were still on hand. True to their word, Braves officials went ahead with the fireworks without any regard for the thousands of unsuspecting people who were sleeping peacefully in their homes near the stadium. Rather than give the survivors of the marathon a free ticket to the next night game and shoot off the fireworks at that time, management sent the bombs bursting in air at 4:01 A.M.

While the fans were oohing and aahing over the boomers, instant terror momentarily swept through the minds of the Braves' stunned, rousted neighbors. One startled citizen dialed 911 and shrieked, "We're being bombed!"

"Lord, there were a few wild minutes there when we thought we had a mini-panic on our hands," recalled Captain C. V. Forrester, of the Atlanta Public Safety Department. "The first thing that was heard was this huge explosion that must have knocked everybody out of bed. People were running out into the streets, some were rushing into our precinct office, and others were jamming our phone lines. Most of the neighborhood thought the Civil War had started all over again."

Then, in a classic understatement, the captain added, "I doubt if anyone went back to bed after that."

Kiteman

Veterans Stadium
April 17, 1972 • April 10, 1973 • April 11, 1980

If ever there was a promotion that just couldn't get off the ground, it was the Philadelphia Phillies' Kiteman.

For the Phillies' home openers in 1972 and 1973, Kiteman—alias Richard Johnson—promised a spectacular act before the start of the game. With roller skates fastened to his feet and a huge kite strapped to his back, Kiteman was supposed to zoom down a 150-foot-long, specially built ramp in the center-field seats, then take off and sail all the way to home plate to present the ceremonial first ball.

But Kiteman was a flop. In his 1972 debut, he roared down the ramp at full speed, but instead of taking off, he veered off the ramp and crash-landed in a heap in the center-field bleachers. "It was just one hell of a crash," said Frank Sullivan, Phillies promotion director. "He went right through the bottom five rows with such force he ripped the seats out. It was unbelievable that he didn't get hurt."

Undeterred, Kiteman returned for another shot the following year. This time, he made it off the end of the ramp—but then nose-dived smack into the outfield warning track. "I don't think he got more than twenty feet off the ramp," said Sullivan.

Kiteman began a tradition of promotional bombs at home openers. The Phillies replaced Kiteman with Rocket Man, who was replaced by Cycle Man, who was replaced by Parachute Man. Other attendance boosters turned sour. The Phillies tried to draw fans by presenting the world's largest jumping Easter Bunny. It was a big rabbit-shaped balloon with a man inside. The balloon was supposed to go about 100 feet into the air and come back down. It got eight feet off the ground.

It was clear that none of the promotions offered the perverse excitement of Kiteman. So in 1980, the Phillies invited him back. But the original Kiteman was nowhere to be found. However, B. J. Beaty was foolish enough to become the new Kiteman. "We brought Kiteman back because he filled the

The Philadelphia Inquirer

stadium for us," explained Sullivan. "It was like the Romans anticipating a good show because they knew they'd get to see the lions tear up the Christians."

This time, Kiteman sailed off the ramp, soared through the air, and made a perfect landing right on home plate. The response from the Philadelphia fans was typical—they booed. Said Sullivan, "It's not all that surprising. In Philadelphia, fans even boo Santa Claus."

Ball Night

Arlington Stadium • April 26, 1986

Texas Rangers fans made it painfully clear that they were more interested in victories than free souvenirs.

A crowd of 25,499, lured by the offer of free official baseballs, were so disgusted over the home team's lousy performance that they decided to give back the giveaway. They hurled hundreds of the balls in anger onto the field, forcing the beleaguered Rangers and umpires to duck and dodge the speeding spheres.

Texas, blasted by the Milwaukee Brewers 11–1 the previous night, looked just as pathetic on Ball Night. On their way to their fifth loss in seven games—a 10–2 shellacking by the Brewers—the Rangers discovered that the fans were not about to be placated by some free baseballs.

In the top of the seventh inning—following a walk, wild pitch, passed ball, two singles, and a homer—the fans unloaded their frustration on the team. First, they started booing loudly. Then someone threw a baseball from the stands. Now here was a creative way to vent their anger, thought the fans. Suddenly, baseballs from all corners of the stadium pelted down on the players and umpires like a hailstorm. Perhaps because they are athletes, the Rangers managed to avoid getting hit by doing some fast stepping. But umpire Tim McClelland wasn't so lucky. He was plunked on the arm by one of the flying balls, but fortunately he wasn't hurt. Enough balls covered the field that the umps stopped the game so the grounds crew could gather them all up.

"It was embarrassing for the state of Texas, a real black mark," declared first baseman Pete O'Brien after the game. "We have a lot of young players trying to grow and learn here this season. We need patience from the fans. What happened made me sick to my stomach. It was very disappointing."

General manager Tom Grieve tried to put the appalling actions of the Ball Night fans in perspective when he said, "At least it wasn't Bat Night."

Baseball Card Day

San Diego Stadium • 1984 and 1985

An annual promotion that seemed as harmless and typical as a hot dog and soda turned into a despicable outbreak of greed and violence at San Diego Stadium.

Elderly fans and little children were knocked down and literally robbed. Not for their money. Not for their jewelry. For their baseball cards!

For years, the San Diego Padres held Baseball Card Day, giving fans free special limited edition sets of Padres' baseball cards. It didn't seem possible that this promotion could cause anyone pain and suffering. But then, team officials never figured that some lowlife adult card collectors would turn into modern-day Fagins who hired gangs of young toughs to wrestle the cards away from fans.

Unlike other giveaways at the ball park, the trading cards attracted not only appreciative card collectors but also money-hungry investors. "These investors—or rather, exploiters—came here with the intention of collecting as many of the cards as possible, and they didn't care how they got them," said Padres marketing director Ron Seaver. "Then they turned around and sold the cards for a profit to avid collectors around the country."

The promotion took a frightening turn in 1984 and 1985 when "investors" assembled teams of muscular, intimidating teenage hoods whose sole mission was to lay their grubby paws on all the cards they could, by hook or by crook.

"These gangs were organized and staked out their own turf at various gates," Seaver said. "They usually wore something that identified themselves— such as a red scarf or a Yankee cap—so that if they bumped into each other, they knew to stay out of the other person's turf.

"As you entered the stadium, they asked you if you wanted your baseball cards. If you said no, they took them. If you said yes, they tried to get them by offering you a dollar or two. If you turned them down, they would hassle you all the way to your seat.

"The real troublemakers tried to steal the cards from fans, especially small children. Little kids with tears in their eyes came up to me and cried, 'Some mean man stole my cards.' I mean, how low can you get?

"These toughs strong-armed elderly fans, too, shoving them around because they wouldn't give up their cards. Why, the thugs even pushed an elderly couple down an escalator in 1985.

"We finally had to draw the line in 1986 and canceled the promotion because our fans were getting hassled and hurt. It's hard to believe that collectors would hire a bunch of teenage thugs to get cards. I guess this is capitalism at its worst."

The Red Sox Witch vs. the Indians' Fairy Godmother

Cleveland Municipal Stadium • May 12–13, 1976

The Boston Red Sox and Cleveland Indians conjured up a bewitching promotion that left the Cleveland fans cursed.

After 10 straight losses, the Red Sox were willing to try anything—even allowing a "witch" to cast a good spell on their bats. A Beantown TV station flew witch Laurie Cabot from Salem, Massachusetts (where else would she live?) to Cleveland, where the Red Sox were opening a three-game series against the Indians. Cabot hoped to end Boston's losing spell by getting the slumping Sox doubles, doubles for their toil and troubles.

"This is pure science," she claimed before attempting her cure in Cleveland. "It has nothing to do with the devil." The witch believed that each person is surrounded by an energy field. Sometimes, on losing teams, the energy field can become dispersed. She was trying to put it back together for the Red Sox.

Wearing a flowing black cape, shoulder-length, jet-black hair, and seven rings on her fingers, Mrs. Cabot appeared on the field just as the Sox started taking batting practice. Not all the Boston players were thrilled to see a witch on the field. "This is a business," grumbled catcher Carlton Fisk. "It's making us look unprofessional."

But teammate Bernie Carbo welcomed the sorceress. He would. In the past, for good luck, he had brought not only a voodoo doll into the dugout but also a stuffed gorilla he called Mighty Joe Young. The witch cast a good spell on Carbo's bat.

Mudcat Grant, who had been throwing batting practice for the Indians, then tried to cancel the witch's magic by putting what he called "the old Lacoochee whammy" on her. He took Mrs. Cabot's hand, looked her right in the eyes, and planted a kiss on her cheek.

Mudcat's whammy didn't work; the witch's spell did. Boston's first batter, Cecil Cooper, bounced an easy grounder that went right through the legs of first baseman John Lowenstein for an error. This was an omen for sure. Cleveland balked across a run, blew a 4–1 lead, and lost 6–4 on three Lowenstein errors. "It wasn't the witch," insisted Lowenstein. "It was simply a matter of incompetence."

The next day, the Indians brought in their own spellbinder. They dressed up former ball girl Debbie Berndt in a white gown and white wig and dubbed her their fairy godmother. Her job was to counteract Cabot's spell.

The fairy sprinkled Cleveland's center fielder Rick Manning with "magic dust." She should have covered his mitt with glue. Manning misplayed one ball into a triple and committed a three-base error on another.

When the fairy godmother left the park in the eighth inning with the Indians well on their way to a 7–5 loss, the fans gave her a tumultuous send-off—of hisses and boos.

Al Smith Night

Comiskey Park • August 26, 1959

Al Smith should have played under an assumed name when his team offered free admission—in his honor—to anyone named Smith.

That's because Al Smith Night turned into Al Smith Nightmare.

From the moment Smith donned a White Sox uniform in 1958, the Chicago fans didn't like him. They were upset over the trade that brought the left fielder to the Sox in exchange for their longtime hero Minnie Minoso. It didn't help matters any that Smith was hampered by a bad ankle and hit only .252 his first year in Chicago. The following year, when the Sox were battling for their first pennant in forty years, Smith had an even worse batting average.

Team owner Bill Veeck decided to help Smith win over the fans by staging a special Al Smith Night. Everyone named Smith was admitted into the left-field stands for free, just by showing some kind of identification.

The idea was great, but the results weren't. Sure, Veeck had the fans *behind* Smith, but that didn't necessarily mean they were *for* him. Throughout the game, all 27,750 spectators, including 5,253 Smiths who were admitted free, booed Smith unmercifully for good reason. He deserved it.

In the game, pitting the first-place White Sox against the seventh-place Boston Red Sox, Smith killed two scoring threats by striking out and grounding into a double play. Things got worse for Smith in the top of the seventh inning. Boston had the tying run on second and no outs when Vic Wertz drove the ball to deep left center. Smith caught up with the ball—then dropped it for an error, right in front of all the Smiths. His flub paved the way for a four-run outburst that vaulted Boston to a 7–6 victory.

Then to cap off the evening, Smith came to bat in the bottom of the eighth with two on and one out. He had the perfect opportunity to atone for his lousy playing and turn the jeers into cheers. The unlucky Smith popped out.

Smith later said he had a premonition that the night might not turn out as planned. Before the game, he went out to the lower left-field stands to sign autographs for the fans named Smith. "I saw my milkman out there that night," Smith recalled. "He was a Polish fellow. So I said, 'How the hell did you get out here?' He said he got hold of somebody's tax bill that had the name of Smith on it. I told him, 'Well, you be my bodyguard out here tonight. I might need one.'"

GOING, GOING, GONE!

Along with the RBI and ERA, baseball should include another statistic—AWOL. Some players would rather play hooky than baseball. They've been known to skip out on the team for a day, a week, or even a whole season. For "The Most Notorious Cases of Players Who Went AWOL," The Baseball Hall of SHAME inducts the following:

Rube Waddell

Pitcher • Pittsburgh–Chicago, N.L. • Philadelphia–St. Louis, A.L. • 1900–1910

Rube Waddell skipped out on his club so many times that he'd be the first choice on any all-time AWOL team.

Although Waddell was one of the best pitchers of his day—he led the league in strikeouts for five straight years and registered a remarkable career ERA of 2.16—he seemed to prefer doing almost anything to playing baseball.

Whenever he disappeared from the team and missed his pitching turn, he was usually found chasing fires, getting drunk, playing marbles, or marching in a parade.

Rube wasted no time in convincing the baseball establishment that he was a free spirit, an impetuous soul who lived life with little regard for the consequences of his offbeat, childlike ways.

He was with the Pittsburgh Pirates only a few short weeks in 1900 before he pulled off his first vanishing act. Slated to pitch against Brooklyn, Waddell was all warmed up and ready. But when the Pirates took the field for their half of the first inning, Rube was nowhere to be found. The umpire notified manager Fred Clarke that if Waddell or a replacement didn't get to the mound right away, he would forfeit the game to Brooklyn.

Clarke sent his benchwarmers on a scouting mission to find the wayward pitcher. Fans told them Rube was last seen leaving the ball park. The search party raced out into the street and found Waddell in his uniform playing marbles with a half-dozen kids.

"Mr. Clarke wants you to come back and pitch," said one of his teammates.

"Tell him I'm busy and to hold up the game until I'm through," Rube replied. Clarke was incensed and personally had to drag Waddell back onto the field where the pitcher proceeded to shut out Brooklyn on three hits.

It was only the first of many Waddell antics that drove Clarke to distraction. More escapades led to more fines. Suddenly, right in the middle of the pennant race, Rube jumped the club and settled in Punxsutawney, Pennsylvania, where he contentedly pitched for the town's team.

In 1902, Connie Mack, manager of the Philadelphia Athletics, thought he could handle Waddell and turn him into a great pitcher. Mack was half right. Obtained by the A's, Rube enjoyed four straight years as a 20-game winner—but he was still just as eccentric as ever.

Once, after Waddell had been missing for two days, Mack and some of his players were standing outside their hotel when they heard a band marching down the street. Leading the band was none other than Rube himself, tossing the baton at least thirty feet in the air and catching it again.

During spring training in 1903 in Jacksonville, Florida, Waddell skipped practice and decided to show off a new and more dangerous skill he'd honed. Mack had no idea where his wacky ace pitcher was until a grimy, rough-looking man approached the manager and said, "I want you to keep that guy Waddell from stealing my stuff. If you don't, you ain't gonna have a pitcher in a few days."

Alarmed, Mack asked, "Well, where is he and what's he doing?"

The man ignored the question. Instead, he pointed to a park down the block and said, "I make my living in that park over there. There's an alligator in that pond and every day at noon I take off my shirt, dive into the pond, wrestle the alligator, and drag him out and then pass the hat. Today that pitcher of yours came over, took off his shirt, and pulled the alligator out himself. Then he went around and collected the money."

Mack spent the rest of the day convincing Waddell that he could make more money throwing baseballs than wrestling gators.

Nothing captivated Rube more than fires and firemen. Before a game in Washington, Mack couldn't find Waddell—until he heard that a nearby building was on fire. Knowing Rube's fascination with fires, Mack hustled over to the scene. But the manager wasn't prepared for what he saw. The first man to poke his head out of the second-story window of the burning building was Waddell, wearing a fireman's hat and carrying a water hose.

Throughout his career with the A's, Rube went on regular benders that sometimes lasted days. The one that caused him the most trouble happened in 1907. Rube stopped at a saloon in Camden, New Jersey, and wound up in a bloody fight. When Mack learned that Waddell had beaten up a tavern patron, the manager decided to take some extraordinary measures to curb Rube's bar-hopping binges.

So Mack framed Waddell in an elaborate hoax pulled off with the tacit approval of the police. The cops "arrested" the pitcher for assault and brought him to a hearing conducted by a police lieutenant dressed up as a magistrate. As the charges were read to Rube, the police led a man swathed in bandages from head to toe into the courtroom.

"Get this man to a hospital immediately!" shouted the fake judge. "He may die on my hands." Then, pointing to Rube, who had turned white as a resin bag, the judge said, "I'm going to put you under $300 bail, make Connie Mack your bondsman, and have a man watch you. If you step out of line again, I'll throw you in jail for six months."

Rube stayed out of trouble the rest of the year and went on to win 19 games.

Rufus Gentry

Pitcher • Detroit, A.L. • 1943–48

As a no-show who held out over a contract dispute, Rufus Gentry really struck out.

It cost him $13,300 to hold out for $1,000.

In the spring of 1945, when major league rosters were weakened by the World War II military draft, Gentry told the Detroit Tigers that he would not sign his new contract unless their $7,000 offer was raised by one grand.

Gentry's demand seemed rather presumptuous considering that he lost more games than he won the previous season, that he led the league in walks, that his ERA was an inflationary 4.24, and that he won only 13 games in his entire major league career.

Detroit management refused to budge from its offer. So Gentry decided he would teach the Tigers a lesson. He failed to report for spring training and began a holdout that all but wiped out his career, not to mention his bank account.

When the season started, Gentry stubbornly remained in Daisy Station, North Carolina, where he lived in a two-room cabin in the hills, ate mostly corn pone and grits, and hunted coons with his hounds.

By midsummer, with both sides still deadlocked, Gentry accepted an offer from a nearby Winston-Salem textile mill to take an easy job at 50 cents an hour and pitch for the company's baseball team on Sundays. Gentry showed up for the first game, retired the first three batters, and then asked the manager what sort of job he was going to have. "Oh, we'll give you an outside job sitting and watching a gate," replied the skipper. Gentry threw down his glove in disgust and said, "I thought you were going to give me an easy job." He quit the team on the spot and returned to the hills, his dogs, and his guns.

Not until August did the Tigers hear from Gentry. By that time, Detroit was making a strong bid for the pennant, and Gentry saw an opportunity to pick up a World Series check. He called the team's general manager, Jack Zeller, and contritely said he was ready to report—albeit five months late. However, Zeller reminded Gentry that it would take at least five weeks to get back in shape for even stop-gap service. "You'd better wait till next year," said Zeller.

There was nothing Gentry could do except read in the newspapers how the Tigers kept winning without him, clinching the pennant on the last day of the season. Detroit then downed the Chicago Cubs for the World Championship. For their share of the World Series payoff, each Tiger received $6,300.

The following spring, Gentry's contract was among the very first signed and returned to the team. "I didn't even look at the figures," he admitted to a teammate. "I just signed the thing and mailed it back."

On the opening day of the Tigers' spring training camp in Lakeland, Florida, Gentry walked forty feet out into left field and stood perfectly still for an hour. The next day, he sauntered fifty feet out into left field and did not stir throughout the entire workout. Manager Steve O'Neill barked at him, "Why aren't you exercising like the rest of us?" Gentry replied, "I've been out a year. I've got to get in shape. You can't expect a man to move too fast so soon."

By holding out for a whole season, Gentry missed out on more than a salary and a World Series check. When the varsity players came marching home from war, he was seldom called on to pitch.

Gentry never started or won another game in the bigs.

Boots Poffenberger

Pitcher • Detroit, A.L.; Brooklyn, N.L. • 1937–39

Boots Poffenberger could pitch, he could hit, and he could field. But most of all he could disappear.

In 1937, only a few short weeks after he had been called up by the Detroit Tigers, Boots pulled off his first vanishing act. Del Baker, acting manager while Mickey Cochrane was out with a fractured skull, called Poffenberger into his office and said, "Boots, we're gonna start you against the Yanks tomorrow."

The rookie pitcher beamed. "That's great. I'm goin' up against the big boys in Yankee Stadium. Boy, that sure makes me happy."

Apparently, it made Boots a little too happy. So elated by the honor paid him, Poffenberger buried his nose in the foam of too much beer that night—and failed to show up for his big start the next day.

A few weeks later in Chicago, Boots missed bed check and was found at 4:00 A.M. leading a swing band at a nearby nightclub. Cochrane deliberately put Poffenberger into the game the next day even though the hung-over pitcher wanted to stay in bed. Like Frosty the Snowman, Boots melted in the hot, muggy afternoon, sweating out everything that ailed him—except his wildness.

Even on occasions when he did make it to his hotel room by curfew,

Poffenberger usually found a way to tick off Cochrane. Team rules stated that players who were not in the hotel dining room by 9:45 A.M. had to pay for their own breakfasts. Boots would arrive at exactly 9:45 A.M., fill himself to the ears with wheat cakes and ham and eggs, and then return to bed for a snooze that often made him late for games.

There was one day he would have been better off staying in bed. Pitching against the Boston Red Sox, Boots enjoyed a comfortable 7–2 lead in the seventh inning. With two out, nobody on base, and two strikes on Bosox player-manager Joe Cronin, Boots got cocky and called him a "showboat." Cronin shouted back, "Take a good look at this park. It's the last time you'll see it. You'll be back with the yokels where a busher like you belongs!" Poffenberger was so teed off that he fired a fastball that nailed Cronin in the butt. Before the inning was over, Boots—who was one strike away from getting the third out—gave up seven runs as Boston racked up ten in the frame and won, 12–7.

Boots, whose given name was Cletus Elwood Poffenberger, finished his rookie year with a 10–5 record and a 4.65 ERA. "If I can win 10 games in the major leagues while staying out at night, imagine how many games I could win throughout a whole season in perfect condition," he said before the start of his sophomore year.

But his good intentions were drowned by Demon Rum. The booze-swigging hurler missed more curfews than a juvenile delinquent and was regularly fined and suspended by Cochrane until the Tigers ran out of patience. Poffenberger, who had a 6–7 mark, was shipped to Detroit's minor league team in Toledo where he finished out the 1938 season.

The next spring, Boots reported to training camp ten days late and got into an argument with Tigers general manager Jack Zeller, who told the bar-hopping, spendthrift pitcher, "The trouble with you, Poffenberger, is you can't handle your money."

Boots replied, "The trouble with you, Zeller, is you never gave me any to see if I could handle it."

That did it. Poffenberger was sold to the Brooklyn Dodgers for $25,000. Although Boots changed uniforms, everything else about him stayed the same.

Boots lasted only three games with Brooklyn. He spent more time in manager Leo Durocher's doghouse than he did at the ball park. The often-fined pitcher missed curfew for the last time on the night of May 23, 1939, in Cincinnati. Although the Dodger train wasn't scheduled to leave until 3:00 A.M., the players were ordered to be in their sleeping berths by midnight. Poffenberger went to his berth at 11:30 P.M. and put on his pajamas. Then, when he thought the coast was clear, he donned his street clothes over his PJs, carefully closed the curtain of his berth, and sneaked off the train. He returned just in time to catch the train—and to catch hell from Durocher.

Boots was fined $400, suspended indefinitely, and then optioned to

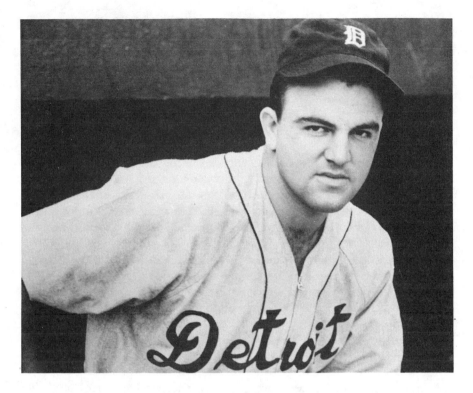

Brooklyn's farm team in Montreal. Four times he told the Dodgers front office that he'd be in Montreal, but he never did find it. He later said that one time he got as far as New York, had a few beers, and then turned around and went back home to Williamsport, Maryland. When the pitcher failed to report to Montreal, baseball commissioner Kenesaw Mountain Landis banned him from organized baseball.

Poffenberger then filed for unemployment compensation. But when all the paperwork was finished, officials couldn't give him any money because they couldn't find him. Boots was missing again.

Pascual Perez

Pitcher • Atlanta, N.L. • August 19, 1982

What's more shameful than losing the game? Losing your *way* to the game.

That's what "Wrong Way" Pascual Perez did on the day he was scheduled to pitch against the Montreal Expos at Atlanta Stadium. What should have been a twenty-minute ride became a three-hour-and-twenty-minute freeway excursion. By the time he arrived at the ball park, Perez was too late and had been scratched from the lineup.

The Braves' rookie pitcher, a Dominican Republic native, had yet to get his bearings in the big city of Atlanta. Since his call-up to the bigs, Pascual had always managed to get a ride to the games. But on the day of his start, Perez decided to drive solo to the stadium for the first time because he had just obtained his driver's license the previous day.

His roommates carefully explained the directions: take Interstate 285 to Interstate 20. What could be simpler? For Pascual, pitching blindfolded would have been easier. He left his apartment at 4:30 P.M., more than three hours before game time. But once he got on busy I-285, a perimeter express-way that encircles Atlanta, he drove, and drove, and drove. After an hour of fighting rush-hour traffic and searching in vain for the I-20 exit, he stopped and asked for directions. But Pascual, who spoke little English, didn't understand them. He remained lost, even after seeking help two more times.

"It's a long way around the perimeter," Perez said later. "The first two times around, I couldn't find I-20. One time I started to get on I-85. I thought that might get me there, but I wasn't sure. So I kept going."

Meanwhile, as game time approached with Pascual nowhere in sight, frantic Braves officials called the Georgia State Patrol, the Atlanta Police Department, and the DeKalb County Sheriff's Office, asking them to search for their missing pitcher.

Perez finally showed up at the stadium at 7:50 P.M., ten minutes after he was scheduled to start. Phil Niekro, who had been slated to pitch the next night, took Pascual's turn on the mound and beat the Expos 5–4.

After hearing Perez's tale of woe, Braves manager Joe Torre fined the hurler $100 for missing his start and then broke up laughing. The next day the team gave Pascual a new warm-up jacket. Instead of his name on the back, it read, "I-285."

Gene Conley   Pumpsie Green

Pitcher   Infielder

Boston, A.L. • July 27–29, 1962

For sheer foolhardiness, nothing has topped the escapade of Gene Conley and his reluctant sidekick Pumpsie Green.

They impetuously skipped out on the team with plans to get away from baseball. Far, far away—to Israel.

The two Bosox were baseball's odd couple. Pumpsie, the first black ever to play for Boston, was a quiet, unassuming utility infielder who was batting only .186. In contrast, Gene was a joking, live-it-up type of guy who had a lot in common with his favorite pitch—both were screwballs. While the compactly built Green did little to distinguish himself on the field, the 6-foot, 8-inch, 225-pound Conley was the Red Sox most consistent pitcher with a 9–10 record. He made a further mark in the sports world by playing pro basketball in the off-season for seven years, including four with the Boston Celtics.

Playing on an eighth-place club in 1962 wasn't much fun for the pair, especially for Gene. He was bushed from playing two sports the year-round and tired of losing several close games.

He reached the breaking point on July 27 in New York when the Yankees shelled Conley for eight runs in the third inning in his poorest effort of the season. After the game, the Red Sox team bus was en route to the airport for a flight to Washington when it was caught in a traffic jam near the entrance to the George Washington Bridge. During the long wait, Gene received permission to leave the bus, supposedly to find a rest room. Somehow, he convinced Pumpsie to accompany him. About twenty minutes later, the traffic jam broke and the bus pulled away without the two players.

Conley and Green found relief not only at a rest room but also at several bars. They had officially jumped the club. While the team was winging its way to Washington, Gene decided that he and Pumpsie should go to Israel. "If we can visit the Holy Land and find God," Conley told Green, "you'll hit .350 and I'll win 20 games."

Although Pumpsie was named after a prophet—Elijah is his real name—he didn't see how a stint in Israel could boost his major league career. After missing a doubleheader, he caught up with the team in Washington and faced the consequences of his truancy—a fine of $500.

Conley, however, persevered. While Bosox officials had no idea of his whereabouts, Gene arrived at JFK Airport (then known as Idlewild). He had his reservation on an El-Al flight to Jerusalem, but with no luggage and no passport, his dreams of Israel faded away. It was just as well. As Conley has since publicly admitted, "I was so tanked up, I didn't have to fly."

So he returned home to his family in Foxboro, Massachusetts, and sent Bosox manager Mike Higgins a telegram that said, "I'm sorry for the way I've handled things but I'm mostly tired and have other plans."

But Gene changed his mind the next day and reported to the club. Taking a dim view of unexcused absences, the Red Sox fined him $2,000. When reporters asked him why he wanted to go to Israel, Conley replied, "I guess I must have thought they had weaker hitters over there."

The front office figured that Gene had already corrupted Pumpsie and would be a bad influence on the younger players. So Green was shipped to the New York Mets and Conley was released early the next year.

Recalled Conley, "I went into a Baptist church and sat in the back row, and halfway through the service, I began to cry. An old man put his arm on my shoulder and said, 'What's the matter, son. Did you lose your mother?' I said, 'No sir. I lost my fastball.'"

WHO ELSE BELONGS IN THE BASEBALL HALL OF SHAME?

Do you have any nominations for The Baseball Hall of SHAME? Give us your picks for the most shameful, embarrassing, deplorable, blundering, and boneheaded moments in baseball history. Here's your opportunity to pay a lighthearted tribute to the game we all love.

On separate sheets of paper, describe your nominations in detail. Those nominations that are documented with the greatest number of facts, such as firsthand accounts, newspaper or magazine clippings, box scores, or photos have the best chance of being inducted into The Baseball Hall of SHAME. Feel free to send as many nominations as you wish. If you don't find an existing category listed in our Baseball Hall of SHAME books that fits your nomination, then make up your own category. (All submitted material becomes the property of The Baseball Hall of SHAME and is nonreturnable.) Mail your nominations to:

The Baseball Hall of SHAME
P.O. Box 6218
West Palm Beach, FL 33405

THE WINNING TEAM

BRUCE NASH continued his long legacy of shameful ballplaying by getting beaned by the pitching machine at an amusement park in his hometown of West Palm Beach, Florida. Nash, a hopeless fan of the hapless Atlanta Braves, once celebrated his birthday by flying his family to Atlanta for a game. The Braves got creamed 19–0. Nash dreams of the day when a player wins the coveted Triple Crown of Shame: most fielding errors, worst batting average, and most game-ending outs.

ALLAN ZULLO was a relief pitcher in high school in Rockford, Illinois—the other team used to sigh with relief whenever he entered the game. His best pitch was a gopher ball and his only asset was a fast outfield. All he knew about good pitching was that he couldn't hit it. As the first player cut during tryouts at Northern Illinois University, Zullo has since lived by the words of Casey Stengel, who once said, "Without losers, where would the winners be?"

Hall of SHAME curator BERNIE WARD learned at an early age he was destined for shame. When Ward showed up for a Little League game as the ninth member of his team, the manager immediately forfeited the game because of a lack of players. In high school in Norton, Kansas, Ward tried out at every position and proved that his limitations were limitless.

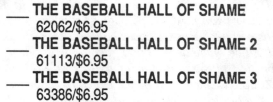